M000249328

THE STORY OF THE WALLOONS

AT HOME, IN LANDS OF EXILE AND IN AMERICA

BY

WILLIAM ELLIOT GRIFFIS, A.M., D.D., L.H.D

Member of the American Historical Association, of the Asiatic and Historical
Societies of Japan and Korea, of Literary and Scientific Societies in the
Netherlands, and of the Société d'Histoire de Protestantisme Belge
Author of "Belgium: The Land of Art," "The Story of
New Netherland," "Belgian Fairy Tales," etc.

WITH ILLUSTRATIONS

BOSTON AND NEW YORK
HOUGHTON MIFFLIN COMPANY
The Riverside Press Cambridge
1923

The Riverside Press
CAMBRIDGE · MASSACHUSETTS
·PRINTED IN THE U.S.A.

JOHANN PRINTZ
Governor of New Sweden, 1643–1653

DEDICATED
TO ALL DESCENDANTS OF THE
BELGIC PILGRIM FATHERS
OF THE
MIDDLE STATES
WHO BY THEIR GIFTS AND GRACES
ENRICHED THE AMERICAN COMPOSITE

PREFACE

THERE are thousands of books on New York and the Middle States — Distinctive America — but in scarcely one, European or American, except in a few local histories, is more than a passing reference made to the first home-makers of the Empire Commonwealth, and in many none at all.

Thirty-one years ago, after seeing in Leyden the records relating to Jesse de Forest, I proposed a memorial in honor of him and his fellow refugees for conscience' sake. He was the potential beginner of the commonwealth of New York, for he was the moving spirit in a colony of Walloons who were the first builders of homes with families and were tillers of the soil of [Terra] Nova Belgica, or New Belgium. This territory comprised the area of our four Middle States, and was so named when given a civic organization in 1626.

These first home-makers in Distinctive America were high-souled pioneers of the freedom of the human spirit and not merely seekers after gain, in fish and furs. They were beginners of the social life of the Middle States, with interests rooted in the soil. I proceed on the principle that men and women, homes and families, are the foundations of a State, and the Walloons began these in 1624. The

vii

PREFACE

trading corporation, called the West India Company, went out of existence in a few years, but the people remained.

Beholding on Manhattan numerous memorials of those who came later — and of many who, in a large sense, were foreigners, that never saw America — while its beginners were ignored, I felt ashamed. Seeing in the archives and in the Walloon Library of Leyden the wealth of documents and data relating to the first settlers of both New England and of the Middle States, I was still further impressed. In the hospitable university city of that Dutch Republic — from which our fathers borrowed the stripes in our flag and so many of our federal precedents, social customs, and inspiring ideas — I noted the multitudinous records of at least four of the great strains in our national composite, English, Dutch, Flemish, and Walloon.

In the company of those free churchmen who first in 1797 were called "Pilgrim Fathers" there were, besides the four nations of the British Isles, four others represented — making a true type of our own mixed people. Before 1873, over five thousand English-speaking students had been educated in Leyden. Possibly a similar total could be counted up in the other "high schools," at Utrecht, Franeker, Groningen, Amsterdam, and Delft.

Besides the city or community archives, I found in the Klog Steeg, across from St. Peter's Church, in the Walloon Library, an astonishing wealth of

PREFACE

records and data concerning these French-speaking exiles, pilgrims and strangers from southern Belgium; for in the Republic were nearly seventy Walloon churches — usually spoken of as "French," because they used that noble language.

Of these records of the neighbors in Leyden of the "Pilgrims" — a name now so honored, yet one which describes with equal accuracy and justice the French-speaking Belgic refugees, called Walloons (or pilgrims) — I have made good use. Several visits in their old home, the southern provinces of Belgium, Hainault, Luxembourg, Liège, Namur, and Brabant, quickened my interest in the story — virtually untold in America — of these who regarded not money, fame, or comfort, but left all, for "freedom to worship God." I visited also most of the cities in Germany to which so many of the Walloons fled, and I hunted up in England several places of worship of these French-speaking Christians, besides reading the records of the larger churches of the Dispersion. To these, and to the publications of the Société d'Histoire de Protestantisme Belge, and the Walloonsche Bibliothek of Leyden, and to many correspondents — Dozy, du Rhieu, Vedder, de Boer, Ravenel, Stoudt, and others, besides our American ministers, consuls, and correspondents abroad — I am much indebted.

Yet even more than by consulting documents, or by reading books, I gladly acknowledge that it was by having lived nine years in Schenectady, amid

ix

PREFACE

many descendants of the Walloons, hearing their traditions, reading the records in their family Bibles, seeing and handling many heirlooms and relics of colonial times, especially in the loan exhibition of 1880, that my imagination was first quickened, and my desire to know more of these "beginners of a better time" became a fixed purpose. Documents and printed matter give one the facts, but not the full truth, and one must have a view from within, of history's "storied windows, richly dight," to appreciate the full effects of these people upon our American civilization.

As I first heard the description of "Old Dorp," from an habitual traveler in Europe, long before it became either the place of my labors or the Electric City, he pictured the Schenectady of 1867 as "an old Flemish town" — an "eddy in the current of American history."

Not only was there a continuous stream of Walloons or of settlers of Belgic stock into this settlement on the Binne Kill of the Mohawk River, from 1661 to 1700 and later, but no fewer than three and possibly four of my predecessors in the pulpit bore Walloon names, or had Belgic blood in their veins. In this town and congregation was reared and thence went forth Dr. Charles Vedder, who, for nearly a half-century, was pastor of the Church of the Huguenots of Charleston, South Carolina, and whose friendship I enjoyed for many years. In Boston, I met Dr. Oliver Wendell Holmes,

PREFACE

who told me of his ancestor who was a deacon in the same church.

In my journey through life, in many countries and cities, I have had pleasant comrades, schoolmates, friends, and acquaintances, whose names, in the perspective of memory, have revealed the fact that they were of either Belgic Walloon or French Huguenot descent. Yet, throughout this book, I have tried to avoid linguistic pitfalls, and have made no statements of fact based alone on the verbal analogy of a name.

I have not attempted a history of the French Huguenots in America, but a sketch of the Belgic Walloons. Nor, with the awful example of some historians before me, have I lost the soul of the story in a mass of antiquarian details. Without any special interest in individual genealogies, but with the purpose of knowing who and whence the American people were and are, have I pursued my search and inquiries.

It is, then, out of the heart, as well as from reading and research — believing that sympathy is the key to interpretation — as an American who feels grateful indebtedness to all who helped in the making of the world's greatest nation and possibly humanity's highest hope, and in the belief that no sectional or sectarian history of the United States can fully or fairly tell our country's story, that this sketch of the pioneers — Belgic Walloons and French Huguenots, who made so rich a contribu-

PREFACE

tion to our national treasury of inheritances — is set forth.

As in the case of the Pilgrim Fathers, who broke the yoke of Norman feudalism and separated Church and State, yet who held the same faith and language, but whose story was occulted by the later and larger immigration of the Puritans, so with the Walloons. They were Huguenots in faith, their native speech was French, and a large part of Belgic Land, long after the Walloon emigration to America, was annexed to France. Hence, in the greater influx, not only of the Dutch and Flemings, but of the French Huguenots in 1690, the story of the Walloons was forgotten. In fame, the one, the Huguenot, increased; while the other, the Walloon, decreased, almost to oblivion.

Yet it may be that art will yet glorify, the pen record, the chisel create, the burin limn, and the inscribed tablet tell, in forms of beauty, of these old facts and truths herein set forth. Politics, governments, rulers, and maps change; but family life, the basis and standard of civilization, perdures, and these people were the makers of homes. The date 1924 may be even more appropriate than 1926 for our Tercentenary and subsequent celebrations. In either or both, it may be well to quote Schiller's line, "Respect him, for he is a Walloon," and to recall that French was the initial speech in the homes of New York, that its colonial laws and scores of church records were kept or published in

PREFACE

this language also, during two generations; and, above all, that the motto of the Walloons was NISI DOMINUS FRUSTRA.

W. E. G.

PULASKI, NEW YORK
May 10, 1923

AUTHORITIES CONSULTED

SPACE does not allow full expression of thanks and grateful obligations to the librarians, archivists, diplomatists, and correspondents in Belgium, the Netherlands, Sweden, Denmark, Great Britain, France, Switzerland, South America, South Africa, and the United States who have freely given aid; but to the late Professor du Rhieu of Leyden; Dr. J. C. Van Dyke, of New Brunswick, New Jersey; Mr. A. J. F. van Laer, archivist, of Albany; Dr. Louis P. de Boer, of Denver, Colorado; and the Reverend J. Baer Stoudt, of Allentown, Pennsylvania, my acknowledgments of obligation are especially due.

Philip Schaff: *Creeds of Christendom.* 3 vols.
Registres de l'Église Réformée Neerlandaise de Frankenthal au Palatinate, 1565–1689.
Publications of the Société d'Histoire de Protestantisme Belge.
Books and pamphlets in the Walloonsche Bibliothek in Leyden.
Various histories of Belgium and the Netherlands — Perrine, van der Linden, van der Essen, Cammaerts, Blok, Putnam, Motley, Hansen, etc.
Bulletins of the Société Belge d'Études coloniales.
D. F. Poujol: *Histoire et Influence des Églises Wallonnes dans les Pays-Bas.*
Jean Martheilhies: *Memoirs of a Protestant (Galley Slave).* Translated by Oliver Goldsmith.
La Cloquet: *Les Artistes Wallons.* Brussels, 1913.
The works of modern writers on Belgium, native and foreign.

AUTHORITIES CONSULTED

J. Winkler: *De Nederlandsche Geschlactsnamen.* 1885.

Nieuw Nederlandsch Biografisch Woordenboek. 5 vols.

L. A. van Langeraad: *Guido de Bray, Zijn Leven en Werken.* 1884.

Register of the Dutch Church in Austin Friars, London (Flemings, Walloons, Netherlanders).

Thirty Thousand Names of Immigrants. Philadelphia, 1898.

Ecclesiastical Records of the State of New York. 7 vols.

Colonial History of New York.

C. Versteeg: *The Sea Beggars.*

C. W. Baird: *History of the Huguenot Emigration to America.*

H. M. Baird: *History of the Rise of the Huguenots.*

L. J. Fosdick: *The French Blood in America.*

F. J. Zwierlein: *Religion in New Netherland* (1623–1664). University of Louvain, 1910.

J. F. Jameson: *Narratives of New Netherland.*

J. W. de Forest: *The de Forests of Avesnes.*

Mrs. R. W. de Forest: *A Walloon Family in America.* 2 vols.

F. V. Goethals: *Dictionnaire généalogique et héraldique des familles nobles du royaume de Belgique.* Vols. i–iv. Bruxelles, 1849–52.

Publications of the Huguenot Societies in England and the United States.

E. T. and C. Corwin: *Manual of the Reformed Church in America.* Five editions.

Various local histories, commemorative discourses, etc., of Schenectady, Albany, Staten Island, New Paltz, New Rochelle, Long Island, and of towns and cities in the British Isles.

Sermons, pamphlets, genealogies, memorial publications, memoirs, biographies, programmes used at commemorative celebrations of Huguenot Walloon churches, in Europe and America.

The authorities used for *Belgium: The Land of Art, The Story of New Netherland,* and *Why Americans should Visit Belgium* (1922).

CONTENTS

xvii

CONTENTS

ILLUSTRATIONS

THE STORY OF THE
WALLOONS

.˙.

CHAPTER I

BEGINNERS OF THE MIDDLE STATES

THE first permanent settlers who, in any number,
came with wives and children to make homes and to
till the soil in New York, New Jersey, Pennsylvania,
and Delaware were Walloons, or French-speaking
people, from the Belgic Netherlands.

Who were they, and why did they come?

Few people from northern Europe, three hundred
years ago, wanted to go and live in America, when it
was a howling wilderness full of savage beasts and
men. A great, wide, stormy ocean had first to be
crossed, and many who made the attempt died on
the way or were massacred when on land. In most
cases, colonization meant starvation. That was the
reason, most probably, why in 1620 the captain of
the Speedwell, which contained by far the better
company of the Plymouth settlers, made a pretext
of leaks and turned back; for the store of provisions
was on the Mayflower. By most people in Europe
the Atlantic had long been considered a Sea of Darkness, and North America the Land of Wild Men. It

was only the West Indies, or South America, where the soil was rich and food plenty, that attracted colonists; but there dwelt the Spaniard, who persecuted. Between the Inquisition and the cannibals there was little choice.

So it was that before men would come with families to what is now the best of all countries, they had to be pushed or driven out from their home lands, like fledglings from the nest. Cruel kings or church rulers must force them to leave their own towns and cities, houses and gardens, before they could think of exile. With most of the first pioneers, it was a choice between prison and torture, being burned alive, or having their heads chopped off.

In distant America were red hunters with tomahawks and scalping knives, who might treat strangers as wild game. Such Americans as then lived here were as ready to roast men alive as were the kings, bishops, and judges of the Europe of that day to send innocent people to the axe, the sword, and the flames. Nor were these benighted red Americans so much to blame, seeing that most white men of that day enticed or hunted the natives with bloodhounds, and made slaves of them. What real difference, then, except in name, between "heathen" and "Christians"?

Their Most Christian Majesties were often worse than Turks or heathen in treating even their own subjects. That is the reason why the brave Netherlanders, called Beggars of the Sea — many of whom

were Walloons — wore a silver crescent, or half
moon, with the motto "Better Turk than Pope."
Henry Hudson in a ship named from the Beggars'
badge and under the seven-red-and-white-striped
flag of the Dutch Republic, entered the rivers Delaware and Hudson, between which are the four Middle States of New York, Pennsylvania, New Jersey,
and Delaware, constituting Distinctive America.
Its first geographical name was New Netherland.
Its first official name was [Terra] Nova Belgica, or
New Belgium — a term that occurs in ancient Latin,
as well as in 1830, when Belgium became an independent state.

Some of us rightly call this region of the four Middle States, Distinctive America; because while from
the first it was more like Europe than any other part
of the United States, it was very different also.
Other colonies followed Old World ideas, denied freedom of conscience and kept Church and State united;
but religion was free in this central region. It was
less like England or France, but more like the Republic of the United Netherlands, where any one
could worship God in the way he wished.

The people of the Middle States were not from
one state or country as were those from the British
Isles who made New England. Before the Revolution, they numbered no fewer than fourteen distinct
nationalities differing in language and forms of religion; but these four colonies formed the first group
that was united under one government and in which

there was toleration for all. When later Governor Stuyvesant played the bigot, he was at once rebuked by the home Government. It was in this Middle Region that the first idea of a union of all the colonies arose; and here was the home of the First Colonial and the First Continental Congress, the Declaration of Independence, the national flag, the Constitution, and most of the ideas and influences that tended to bind the separated colonies in federal union under one government, infused with one soul as a nation.

There never was any such country or place called New Netherlands. In naming geographically, in 1614, the new American province of the Dutch Republic, New Netherland, and politically [Terra] Nova Belgica, the Dutch West India Company followed the example set by one of the best men who ever lived. This was William the Silent, called the Father of his Country, and the ancestor of Queen Wilhelmina. When his baby daughter was born, he had her christened at Antwerp and named Catherine Belgica. William hoped that all the seventeen provinces of the Netherlands would be united in one republic and under one flag, with liberal ideas as to religion, that is, freedom of conscience guaranteed to all; and he very nearly succeeded in realizing it. The Dutch federal flag, from which we borrowed the stripes in ours, consisted of seven alternate bands of color, white and red, representing commonwealths, not individual rulers.

4

BEGINNERS OF THE MIDDLE STATES

William wanted seventeen stripes, as earnestly as our forefathers in 1775, led by General Washington and Dr. Benjamin Franklin, hoped for fourteen stripes in ours, by having Canada in the federation, for this province had been represented in the first Continental Congress of 1774. In America, Puritan New England opposed toleration in Canada. We need not wonder at this, when politics and religion were considered as one and inseparable. In Ghent, fanatics on one side were just as bad as those on the other, for the Calvinists burnt monks and priests alive.

In the Union of Arras (now in France), in 1578, the Belgic Netherlands separated from the Dutch. Then the flag of the Republic had only seven stripes. Yet often the republican battle flag consisted of twenty-one stripes, that is, the red, white, and blue seven times repeated.

It is both fact and truth to assert that those who most persecuted men for their conscience' sake helped powerfully to effect the colonization of America. This is confessed even in memorials to the persecutors. For example, some English people put up a stained glass window in the church at Stratford-on-Avon, in which Shakespeare is buried. The inscription says that Archbishop Laud "promoted the colonization of America." But how? In the same way that Philip II, the King of France, and the Pope did. All were men of their time. They did not think as rulers do now, and they all supposed they were doing right. It had been the old way and they followed in the footsteps of their fathers, fearing the wrath of Heaven if they departed from it. Unconsciously they were as sons of Jacob and brothers of Joseph.

Laud thought that people who did not think as he did should be robbed, imprisoned, put to death, or driven out of the country. So did Louis XIV, the King of France. So also did the Queens, Mary and Elizabeth. Exiled from their home land, English fathers and mothers, as early as 1555, called themselves pilgrims and gave to more than one child the name Peregrine, as was later done on the May-flower. King James I and his feudal bishops drove out the thinking people, thousands of whom took refuge first in the Dutch Republic, where "religion was free for all men" — later enriching America at the expense of England. Thus the monarchs of Spain, France, and England "promoted the coloni-zation of America."

It is all so very different now — for we live in a new world of thought — that we must ask, "Why were these rulers of Church and State so cruel and bitter against innocent people, who had done no wrong, neither committed any crime?" Were those "commanded to leave the realm" bandits or murderers?

These rulers themselves would be thought such if they lived to-day, but three hundred years ago, the ideas and customs of both "Christians" and "hea-then," in Asia and in Europe, were very much alike in one respect. The gentlemen who sat on thrones and wore crowns, and those in miters and lawn sleeves, were pretty much of one mind in their policy. If any man held a different opinion from theirs he was considered an outcast and worthy of death. Non-conformity was a crime. Was it China, or India, or Europe, that was in a state of arrested development? Probably Marco Polo thought the latter.

Because it is all changed now in most countries of the world, we are not to abuse thoughtlessly the men of different minds in old days, or judge them by the moral standards of to-day. It is only by putting out of our minds the present ruling ideas and entering into "the spirit of the age" in which they lived, that we can do them justice, even while grateful for those who, seeing beyond the immediate troubles, were faithful to their intelligent convictions.

CHAPTER II

WHO WERE THE WALLOONS?

ON the islands of the Manhattan archipelago, and at places along the Hudson and Delaware rivers, the Walloons made their settlements, beginning in 1624. As pious and high-souled as the Pilgrims, they had on board their vessel a church officer, who led song and worship. In later years, thousands more of these Belgian people came over in the ships. Probably two thirds of the inhabitants of New Netherland, called "Dutch," were from the southern or Belgic part of the seventeen provinces — Flemings who spoke Dutch and Walloons whose speech was French; but all held the Reformed Christian faith based on the deathless literature found in the Bible. In religion, the "Walloons" from Belgium and the "Huguenots" from France were one, as were the Pilgrims and Puritans.

As to the territory of the Walloons, in the political shiftings of feudal and later times, part of it was sometimes in France, again in Belgium, and still again in France. This may explain why the spiritual life of Belgic Walloons and French Huguenots was much the same.

In the case of both the Pilgrim and the Walloon, the story of the smaller company was first occulted and then lost in that of the larger body. Myriads can be seen more easily than hundreds — the forest sooner than the trees — but now the story of both has been recovered for American history, while in Holland the Walloon story never was lost. In 1668, by the Treaty of Aix-la-Chapelle, confirmed in 1713 by that of Utrecht, a large part of Walloon Belgium, or the "Spanish Netherlands," was ceded to France, and from this district, now in the Département du Nord, came a large part of the Huguenot emigration, which after this date helped to people America.

In the new American province of the Dutch Republic, the hardy male pioneers who fished in the waters, or with the Indians bartered trinkets for furs, guns, and textiles, or explored the land, during the fifteen years from Henry Hudson's time, or from 1609 until 1624, were almost wholly Dutch. They had no homes, for they were without wives or children, nor did they till the soil. They made money and maps, and one, whose name is in Cape May, New Jersey, built a small ship called the Onrust, or Restless. It was a hunter and swift-goer, or, in Dutch, a "yacht." Some lived in huts over a winter, and even, it may be, that men with wives and children made brief visits, but they did not have homes, orchards, fields, gardens, cattle, poultry, or title to the land. No guaranteed legal land tenure or ownership of the soil was possible until after the West India Company was formed in 1621.

The Walloons made of the wilderness a new home land. They did not call themselves at first "Walloons." This was the term applied to them when they had lived in a foreign land. It was as with the "Pilgrim Fathers," who were never so called until the year 1797. A foreigner in Antwerp, the Englishman Gresham (ancestor of our former Secretary of State) in 1567, first in the English language, spoke of "the Vallons."

These people were probably among the descendants of the Belgæ, of whose ancestors Cæsar, the Roman general, tells us. He declared that they were the bravest of all the tribes. They were proud of being one of the oldest people in northern Europe. On the first official seal used on New York soil, we read Sigillum Novi Belgii, and [Terra] Nova Belgica was the name of the new land. Both Batavia (meaning better land), and Belgica, or Belgium, were used much as we use the word "Columbia" for America.

The settlement on Manhattan, which means "a place between two rivers," was called by them, though never officially, New Avesnes or Avennes, the birthplace of their leader, Jesse de Forest. Moreover, the first language spoken in the homes of Distinctive America, or the Middle Region, was French. We shall tell about the adventures of the Walloons of America in this book; but first we shall look at them on their native soil and learn of their flight and fortunes in several lands, and how they got across the Atlantic. Environment dictated their development through the centuries, but heredity showed what was in them to do. Their history is well worthy of study. From the Walloons in the Belgium of to-day, these early makers of New York differed chiefly in matters of conscience.

Take the map of Belgium and draw a line from west to east, through Brussels. South of this are the provinces of Hainault, Namur, Luxembourg, and Liège. These are called the Walloon provinces, or, of late, "Walloonia"; for now the people and the government have accepted and are proud of the name, just as we are of that of the once unknown "Pilgrim Fathers." The name Walloon, which has nothing to do with the Waal (inner or turbulent) River, or the imaginary single province of "Walloonia," helps us to distinguish these people from the Flemings, of the northern half of Belgium — the country which has two races, two languages, two centers of industry, two landscapes, and two varieties of religion. To-day the old Walloon district includes also the Département du Nord in France, which was once part of Belgium.

Yet from the first beginnings of language, the root-word *wal*, with its variations in spelling and pronunciation, meant alien, stranger, foreigner. The Romans called all the northern people by such a word (Wealsh or Welsh), even as the Germans so speak of the Italians to this day. In Belgic Land, while "the Franks settled in the North, the Romanized Celts or 'Walas' occupied the South." Later on when church dioceses were formed, men spoke of the "Walas" and "Dietschen" — Celts and Germans.

THE STORY OF THE WALLOONS

When we look further into the use of this root word, we find it not only in Switzerland in the canton of Wallis, in the Netherlands in the island of Walcheren, in Britain applied to the Cymric Land of Wales, but we also discern it in hundreds of English and American place-names, such as Walton, Wallingford, etc. In Dutch, to say of a man "he speaks Waalsch" (Welsh) means he is a Walloon, or he speaks French.

This division of Belgium means more, also, than in race and speech. The Flemings are farmers, the Walloons are mechanics. North Belgium is agricultural, South Belgium is industrial. At Louvain, the traveler bids good-bye, once for all, to everything Flemish. The town halls and cathedrals, that is, civic and religious architecture, are not in the same style. The scenery is different. Flanders is flat; the Walloon country is rich in hills. To live in Louvain and in Ghent is much like dwelling in two worlds. The peasant from Hainault when in Flanders is in a foreign land, nor can he feel at home. Brussels, the capital in Brabant, is the meeting place of language and race. Into it the riches of north and south are poured. This city is a smaller Paris.

Yet both Walloons and Flemings are intensely patriotic, for they have been united in one nation for over five hundred years. They have the same kind of money, they follow the same way of living, and are proud of their history. Instead of being ground to powder between the two millstones of France and

WHO WERE THE WALLOONS?

Germany, the Belgians have never been wholly crushed.

How much of the Teutonic strain is mixed in that of the Walloon is a question probably never to be settled. Many foolish notions persist and theories have been spun from the exaggeration of the original race element or subsequent admixture in the Walloon. The astonishing thing is that these two races and languages have remained intractable to all attempts to mix them; yet in friendliness and even in patriotism the Belgians have ever been one, thus furnishing a noble example to mankind in general and a rebuke to all who hate "foreigners."

Nine tenths of the real or imaginary divisions or estrangements noticeable in their history have had little or nothing to do with language, nor were they racial, but almost wholly economic. In fact, as a rule, foreigners exaggerate the ethnic and linguistic divisions, while native historians, like Perrine, show us the reality. The last signal attempt to separate Walloon and Fleming — to rend a nation asunder — by an appeal to race and language, was made by the invaders of 1914. Like all previous similar efforts to destroy Belgium, it failed miserably. There was an eternal Belgium long before 1830.

The most interesting part of Belgic Land to the tourist is in the North, the most beautiful scenery in the South. For nearly a thousand years, there have been three industrial centers — of textiles, of metal working, and of trade; that is, Flanders, Walloon

Land, and Antwerp — each excelling in its special products.

Why did so many of the southern Belgians, from 1567, leave their beautiful land? Why, but for conscience' sake and loyalty to the Highest! In England, they were treated rather roughly by the apprentices and workmen, who were jealous of their superior abilities in craftsmanship. Borrowing the word from the Dutch, these Englishmen called them "foreigners" — "wall" meaning alien and "oon" meaning one, that is, a foreign fellow, a stranger. They were twitted with leaving their country and not fighting hard to defend it. Yet an American engineer and soldier — one of the million or more descendants of the first Walloons in New York — has given his judgment that the Belgic or Walloon region is not militarily defensible.

Belgium has no great natural frontiers. Her territory is open on all sides. Nevertheless, for half a millennium the dragons, whether French, or German, or Dutch, have failed to swallow her. Every one of the numerous wars and invasions, even down to 1914, has confirmed the American engineer's opinion. After millions spent on General Brialmont's system of fortifications, the Germans took both the Liège and Antwerp forts. Of all Belgium, the Walloon portion has usually been the most devastated.

The first martyrs, in the new era of Bible study, two young monks, Esch and Voes, were burned alive, in the public square in Brussels. The Wal-

WHO WERE THE WALLOONS?

loons are very quick to catch a new idea, and hence they promptly welcomed the Reformation; but when death was pronounced against them, by the royal Spaniard in the Escurial, the order to change their ways of thinking came so suddenly that they had neither the time nor the power of defense. Against the large and finely disciplined and equipped army of Alva that in 1567 invaded their country, they were helpless.

The men of the new mind wanted to read the Book of books. Philip II and his bishops said: "No, you cannot, you must think as we think, worship as we worship, and read only what we permit you; or we shall drive you out of the land, or kill you." Hence the flight and dispersion of the Huguenot Walloons in all the countries of the Reformation, from Sweden to Russia, in South Africa and South America, and in the Dutch and English colonies of North America.

In our day and country, people can think and read what books they please, and worship God in their own way, too, if they obey the law. But three centuries ago, it was the general custom with most governments, heathen, Confucian, Mahometan, and Christian, to imprison, hang, burn, or behead people of the other party. So long as the lust of power, place, and pelf rules in men's minds, this will be so; for men hide their animal passions under the cloak of religion. History shows that in any age and country, all over the world, those who claim to be vicars of God, and have the power, will persecute. History also shows that in most cases "orthodoxy" means success and "heresy" defeat. Grant the first premise, of monopoly of authority from Heaven or God, given to persons, parties, or corporations, and all their claims logically follow, whether in Asia, Europe, or Africa.

Philip II of Spain, who had terrible quarrels also with the Pope, thought he was serving God when he sent the Duke of Alva to behead nobles, whether of the old or the new form of the faith, to hang innocent people, to confiscate their property, and to depopulate and desolate the land. At his proceedings we shall look, while we tell the story of the Walloons. If we know what happened in the past and learn the story of human progress, we shall be all the more thankful for the country and the times in which we live. We shall understand all the better our own history and government, for even nations and the whole human race are pilgrims ever marching onward and, though with many a setback, moving forward. "The dogs bark, but the caravan moves on." That is the picture of human progress.

CHAPTER III

HOW THE NATIONS OF EUROPE WERE FORMED

EUROPE is the magic mirror whose history reveals to us our own national story. The struggle for liberty in America was but that of adjournment from the old to the new continent. Even the American Revolution, rightly interpreted, is but one of the glories of English history.

In our age of the world, when we speak of Frenchmen, Germans, Italians, British, Dutch, or Belgians, we think also of certain countries on the map, with boundaries, with the people in each as speaking a particular language, and usually one language only. Besides this, in a general way we all picture to ourselves the kind of a man he is whom we call a Britisher, a Dane, a Swede, a Frenchman, an Italian, or a Russian.

In a similar way even in our country we think of New England and Yankees, of the South and Southerners, of the Middle West, the Far West, and the Pacific slope, and the people in these sections. The United States being as large as Europe, we divide also the time. So we have for our railroads Eastern, Central, Western, and Mountain time. We are vociferous in shouting "Progress" as a battle-cry, yet this idea of progress is a modern one. Those who three or four centuries ago urged it were under ban as heretics and malefactors.

A thousand years ago even the idea of nationality was but faintly apprehended in Europe, and we may say much the same of the different literatures and boundaries. Nor were most of the words which now describe the great nations and peoples in use, or even conceived of. Most persons never went more than a few miles from home. It was only in war time, or for commerce, that a few Europeans moved. In the Far East, however, travelers had the magnetic compass and used it on land and sea. Sailors ploughed the ocean and caravans traversed mountains and plains. What most of our books call "the history of the world" refers almost wholly to countries around the Mediterranean — the very name of which exposes the ignorance of ages.

The inhabitants of middle and northern Europe had been from very early time wandering tribes of savages, or barbarians. The civilized peoples were the Greeks and Romans, who dwelt along the Mediterranean, or Middle-Earth Sea. The Romans, in their course of kingdom, republic, and empire, during twelve hundred years, pushed their way north as far as the Rhine river and in Britain almost to Scotland. In large measure the Roman Empire thrust itself between the tribal emigrations, stopped their wanderings, and, until the fifth Christian century, kept them in check. Then the northern barbarians — the "Waalsch" — who already composed over half of the soldiers and slaves, destroyed the Empire. Thus Rome fell, as much from internal decay as from external attack.

For several hundred years, until the ninth century, there were hordes, clans, and tribes moving about, fighting, conquering, and settling in new lands and upon other people's territory, but there were not as yet the states and their boundaries with which we are familiar on the map.

The man who, after the ruined Roman Empire, tried to unify Europe by restoring order was Charlemagne; that is, Carolus Magnus, or Charles the Great, of Walloon Land. Born in the Belgic village of Herestal, in the year 742, he lived until A.D. 814. His model, the only one he thought possible, was in the past; but the name of the new political structure was the Holy Roman Empire. For seven centuries onward, the two great forces shaping history were Papal and Imperial, Pope and Emperor, the Church and the Empire.

To most of the tribes in northern Europe that still worshiped gods, whose names are recalled in the days of the week, Charlemagne was like a hammer. He made of them what were called "Christians," by first overcoming them in battle and then driving them by thousands, at the point of the spear, into the rivers to be "baptized." Then, accepting the faith, they were at least churchmen, if not followers of Jesus. To accomplish his purpose, he transplanted colonies of them along the North Sea, whither others had fled before his arms, and so were called "fleemings" or Flemings.

On Christmas Day, A.D. 800, Charlemagne was in Rome, and the Bishop of that city — the Papa or Pope — placed a crown on the warrior's head. This signified the union of Church and State, the joining of spiritual and temporal power; which meant, in practice, that Christianity could be propagated by force, like Mahometanism. This act and what followed logically from it directly reversed the Founder's teaching.

From this time, the sword and battle-axe and the shepherd's crook, or crozier, went together. "The Holy Roman Empire" influenced European politics for nearly a thousand years. The underlying idea was that the "whole world" — of which only a small portion was known in Europe — belonged to all who were churchmen, or "Christians." The "heathen" had no rights which rulers or people called Christians were bound to respect. This great religious corporation in Italy compelled kings and emperors to obey its decrees. In spirit, it was as far as possible from what the Founder said, when He declared before the Roman governor, "My kingdom is not of this world; if my kingdom were of this world, then would my servants fight." As to the length of its existence, Charlemagne's has been well called a "mushroom empire." Its story was soon told.

As used in European politics, the idea that Church and State were one has been above all others the

cause of innumerable wars and bloodshed. For five
or more centuries this dogma, almost unchallenged,
except here and there by sects, ruled the European
nations in their evolution. It taught that the ruler
of a country, or the local magistrate, had a right to
lord it over the conscience, and that the State could
dictate the religion. From this grew up the motto,
when Latin was the common language of the learned
and of rulers and documents, *cujus regio, ejus religio;*
that is, whose is the region, his is the religion. He
who governed the country could say what people
were to think and believe. So in France and Belgium, "the King's religion" was held to be the only
real one, while that based on the Bible was officially
dubbed the "Pretended Reformed Religion."

Moreover, the king, or governor, could carry out
his will by force, fire, and sword, even dealing out
death to the men who did their own thinking. Such
a system was at the antipodes of what Jesus taught,
"My kingdom is not of this world."

Rome was thought to be the center of the (flat)
earth. Hence all authority must proceed from the
city on the Tiber, where the capital of the Roman
Empire had been. This was exactly like the Chinese
dogma of Whang Ti, which supposed that the Emperor of China was God's vicar and the Chinese nation was the most civilized in all the earth, and that
all authority, spiritual and temporal, must proceed
from the capital. Hence the long-continued persecutions in China, which the great Dutch scholar,

de Groot, has revealed to us. Both forms of the same notion, Chinese and Roman, which invariably meant persecution, are now perhaps becoming obsolete, though they are still a menace to ordered freedom.

Such a system seemed necessary in the days of darkness and ignorance, when only monks and priests could read and write, and when the Church did a mighty work in unifying and instructing the nations. General education was not as yet thought of, and the Bible was unknown to the masses. In our time, with free public schools, such a doctrine is so far out of date that it is only by isolating people from infancy and filling their minds with ideas unknown in the Book of books, that such a monopoly of religion can be perpetuated. We shall see what forces broke up this one of the several feudal systems, and brought in the new age which we enjoy.

When Charles the Great died, in 814, he had no son who was capable of ruling the vast realm; but in the third generation there were three grandsons, who agreed to divide the empire, each taking an equal portion. The ceremonies of partition, with the sacred oaths, sworn to by each of the three princes, were solemnized in A.D. 843, at a place in France called Verdun — the same where, over a thousand years later, the waves of German invasion were rolled back in defeat.

The scope of this mediæval compact included even more than geography and politics. From this date, the languages, the literatures, the nations, and the modern states began to form and their boundaries to be fixed. Roughly speaking, the West was France, the East, Germany. The central state, made up of the border lands of western Europe, extended from the English Channel to Italy. It included Belgic Land, and was named the Kingdom of Lothair, or Lotharingia. Henceforth, in history, we recognize Frenchmen, Germans, Italians, Spaniards, Englishmen, etc.

Nor in the category of European nationalities can Belgium — "the great little country" — be left out, nor the Belgians be ignored; for no other country has survived greater changes and the attempts of many mighty potentates to absorb or destroy her. The short-lived Kingdom of Lothair, formed by the Verdun Compact of A.D. 843, between France and Germany, still lives in Belgium, as the barrier between France and Germany, for the good of civilization.

Even from Roman times nature assisted. The Coal Forest, stretching from east to west across the entire country, broke the invaders' efforts and enabled Belgic Land to gain an independence she has kept — despite occasional loss of sovereignty — as "the last fragment of the great empire of Lothair."

In a large sense, the political movements of human society are like the pendulum of a clock. They swing first toward unity and then separation; in the direction of empire and again of self-determination.

THE STORY OF THE WALLOONS

Centralization and independence make up the story of nations equally in Asia and in Europe.

From the ninth century, European society was formed on a new basis, which was neither Roman nor barbarian, but feudal. Feudalism was as a great school, and most of the nations went through its long discipline. Its moral foundation was the law of contract, of mutual obligation.

This system of society, based on land tenure, changed the landscape, giving new edifices, such as the castle, monastery, tithe-barn, with village unity of crafts, and the cathedral, in which all spiritual life centered. The knight and man-at-arms, the monk and friar were the two outstanding types of superior men above the masses. They were looked upon as the models, which fathers and mothers wanted their sons to copy. Although the prelates lorded it over the common people, the Church, in the main, was the nurse of democracy; for any boy could become a monk, a priest, a bishop, or a pope, although in later times the papacy became in the main an Italian monopoly.

Yet besides the shaping of nations and countries in both their boundaries and their interior constitutions, through the human hand and brain, we must not forget those influences of nature which are powerful and continuous. As there are several theories in philosophy and theology as to the genesis or genealogy of the human soul — apart from the body — so there are sound and unsound theories as to the origin, causes, and continuous reason for the existence of Belgium and the two types of humanity within her borders. Cloquet, in strongly arguing, as against Maeterlinck, that the Walloon genius has been richly productive of painters, as well as sculptors and architects, tells us that "in the old Italian writings we find the term *flamminge Vallone* (Flemish–Walloon) which well characterizes the confusion which results from mixing indiscriminately the reputation of the two races."

Lest the body and soul of Belgium be imagined to be but a patchwork, made on the green baize table of European congresses and diplomatists, let us, with Emile Cammaerts, look at the efficiency of unwearied nature in producing di-ethnic and bi-lingual Belgium, which is among the oldest of nations.

During the period from the Roman occupation to the era of the Crusades, one notable change was made in the landscape, which profoundly affected government, language, social development, and both local and international politics. It fixed permanently the dualism of race and speech. It stereotyped what is most peculiar to bi-lingual and di-ethnic Belgium. Side by side, but immiscible, are the Walloons and Flemings.

By a paradox, the long, slow, gradual, almost imperceptible process of removal or deforestation, while it made permanent separation of speech and blood, developed a national consciousness, uniting the two ethnic elements into one people and awakening patriotism. The Charcoal Forest, which the Romans never penetrated and around which their roads ran east and west, whether living or eliminated, has determined the history of the Belgians.

The Latin world rulers divided their northern conquests between the Seine and the Rhine into Belgia Secunda — that is, Lower Belgium, in which was the hill region of the Ardennes and the great Silva Carbonaria, or Charcoal Forest — and Germania Inferior. The Roman highroad ran north of the great woods from Cologne to Arras and westward even to the Seine. The invading Franks settled in the North, the Romanized Celts or "Walas" (Walloons) occupied the South.

This Charcoal Forest extended all the way over the distance which the great highway traversed. The Romans made use of the iron in the mines and improved the art of smelting the ore, manipulating the metal by using charcoal. Hence the name they gave to the forest, which neither they of old nor, at first, even the Franks penetrated. It served to isolate the Walloons. In the later onslaughts of the Germanic tribes, the natives found shelter and defense in this wood's recesses.

Parallel in both time and space, in Britain the Teutonic tribes drove the natives westward into the Cymric forests and then called them by the same name, Walas, or Welsh; that is, foreigners. Geology and history clasp hands. The same rocks form alike the hills of the Ardennes and the mountains of Wales.

HOW THE NATIONS WERE FORMED

In time, however, the last waves of Teutonic paganism "spent their force along that leafy barrier which saved Christianity and Roman civilization and incidentally gave the Belgian nation its most prominent and interesting character. The singsong of a Walloon sentence may thus suggest the rustling of the leaves and the piping of the early birds, while the more guttural accents of a Flemish name remind us of the war cry of wild hordes and the beating of lances."

It was the cutting down of this forest, first on its western and southern sides, while the northern and eastern flanks remained comparatively untouched for centuries, that brought the Walloons into closer intimacy with the Franks. By speech and common intellectual and economic interests, the French and Southern Belgians were thus linked together in the same aims and interests.

Yet before fire and the axe had erased from the landscape the Coal Forest, the Walloons in the neighborhood of Liège had early in the fifteenth century become famous all over Europe for their skill and varied craftsmanship chiefly in iron, but notably in other metals. This reputation they have never lost, and we shall, in our narrative, see to whom and what Sweden owes her wealth in iron.

CHAPTER IV

HOW ASIA ENRICHED EUROPE

IN modern electric science, by the use of the alternating current, men have accomplished great results, while it has revealed wondrous possibilities. In human history, also, we discern a stream of mutual benefit flowing from the pendulum-like motions of advance and retreat, as the civilizations of East and West touch each other. Some see only the clash of war, or what are apparently the evil results; others behold beneficent reactions. In its frequent recurrent devastations and re-creations, Belgium's history seems like an alternating current.

In what we call the Middle Ages there were two great waves of movement and enterprise, both of them notable for their influence on the whole race. The first was westward and the second eastward, and by these both of the two continents and great religions powerfully affected each other. These series of events were the rise of Mahomet and the Saracens, as against the Crusades, and the capture of Jerusalem by the Crusaders. In the campaigns of men fighting under the crescent and the cross, Belgium had a notable part, for like Charlemagne, Godfrey de Bouillon, King of Jerusalem, was from Walloon Land.

Through these movements, men of different

creeds, races, and minds became acquainted with each other and with the world in which they lived. Out of Christian knighthood arose chivalry and romantic love between man and woman. Fine manners became more and more the rule of life, while in the homes of the European peoples, especially at the seaports and in large cities, and in the houses, orchards, and gardens, were new things to eat, to see, to use, to wear, and to enjoy, which had come from the East. Dress, painting, architecture, manners, and methods of business were all affected by this mutual contact of races. To what extent in the domain of external religion there was mutual borrowing is a question, but it is certain that Buddhism and the Roman form of Christianity made many exchanges.

These effects are notably discernible in wall paper, faience, carpets, tapestry, and oil painting. The wonderful colors of the Van Eycks, on wood and canvas, were suggested by the Oriental miniature paintings. The passion of the East is decoration, that of the West form. In Belgium, the land of art, the charms of both were blended. Printing, gunpowder, porcelain, wind-mills, banks, jewels, precious stones, falconry, the mariner's compass, and a host of Asian inventions and luxuries, from the loom, the garden, the orchard, and the farm, enriched Belgic Land.

The stimulus to commerce and industry was immense. New trades and products raised the standard of living in both the castles and the humbler dwellings. Commerce created a prosperity that made the Belgic Netherlands the richest part of Europe and the envy of kings and nobles. The cloth, the lace, the tapestry, the pictures, both woven and painted, the stories in the Bible and in the classics of Greece and Rome represented on canvas and in textiles, became famous all over Europe and in other lands and on continents afar.

Hitherto Asia, the Mother Continent, had been much wealthier than Europe, for most of the inventions, the finer things of life, fruits and flowers, strange birds and animals, articles of food and drink, spices and condiments, luxurious clothing and other products of the loom, with many of the sports, amusements, fairy tales, and legends now common among us, came from India or China. In time, tea, coffee, and the whole line of hot drinks adorned the European table and gave woman her proper place at the head of it. Surprising novelties and a thousand wonders, unknown in Europe before, seemed to make a new world.

Before the Crusades, these novelties had been for the most part brought overland by caravans. It is very interesting to trace out on the map the old routes of travel. At the ends of this land traffic, in Italy and France, immense wealth was accumulated by the merchants in the great fairs. It was mainly from the money made by this lucrative land commerce with Asia, together with the sale of indulgences, that those miracles of human genius, the mighty cathedrals of southern and central Europe, were reared.

Two series of events changed this stream of wealth and abolished the land routes, beginning a new era of trade by sea. The Italian Marco Polo had been to China, and on coming back told of its vast wealth and high state of civilization. By the Chinese magnetic needle, used as the mariner's compass, men could now sail out of sight of land and into the distant seas. What seemed to be the finger of God, directing them how and where to go, made men bolder and led to the discovery of new routes over the ocean to the rich Indies, Java, China, Korea, and Japan. Undreamed of forms of wealth, like tidal waves, rolled in upon southern Europe.

Then followed also the unveiling of continents and the discovery of America, which not only meant new riches to Europe, but made even a greater gift to the human imagination. The process so enlarged men's minds that boundless possibilities loomed. In their wonder they called the new continent the New World.

Humanity had gained new horizons. The earth seemed made over again. Western Europe learned also about Oriental civilizations and of another "Catholic" Church, which used the Greek instead of the Latin language in worship and had the New Testament in the tongue of the apostles. In the Western Church, discipline and the centralization of power upheld by force were the characteristics. In the Eastern Church, doctrine and philosophy were the prevailing features. The Latin and the Greek mind worked in contrast.

Compared to those of the South, the northern countries of Europe were not only colder, but much poorer. Something now happened which made even England and Sweden co-heirs to the immeasurable good fortune which contact with Asia had brought.

In 1453, the Turks captured Constantinople. Islam, or the religion of Mahomet, swept even into India and China. After this, the overland trade by caravans ceased, because the Turks had closed the passage, so that transit from the Orient to Europe must henceforth be by sea. Between Bagdad and China were high mountains. The Arabs, therefore, made their voyages to the Far East, Java, China, and Korea — as the Arabic geographer Khordadbey records — in ships. We have also the record of the Chinese fleet sailing in 1122 from Ningpo in China to Korea, and directing its course by the magnetic compass. It was during the Middle Ages that Korea was in her high splendor of civilization, while Japan was relatively in anarchy and barbarism. This change in the old trade routes and the caravan business had at first brought fleets of ships and the profits of Oriental commerce to the cities along the Mediterranean Sea, pouring into the lap of Florence, Rome, and the ports of the Italian republics, riches beyond all former dreams; but later, it was the making of Belgic Land. The cities of Flanders were full of weavers, lace- and tapestry-makers, besides merchants and bankers from many lands. Later, Antwerp became the chief seaport of all Europe and one of the richest cities in the world, largely because of this shifting to the northward of the trade routes. Even then, without the submarine cable, or radio, the ends of the earth had met.

The people in flax land, that is, the Walloons, profited also; for in the making of lace, tapestry, and linen textiles, flax, one of a thousand gifts of Asia to Europe, was of the first importance. In the springtime the southern provinces seemed to mirror the empyrean, for their area became a vast field of blue flowers. In the autumn, thousands of stacks of stalks, each one filled inside with the glossy silk-like fiber, fed thousands of looms of weavers; or the silvery white strands lay on the pillows at which the lace-makers, male and female, were constantly busy. The strands used in the finest lace, wrought and workable only in cold and darkness, seemed a mirror of the history of Belgic Land — so often the home of sorrows, yet so many times again rising into beauty and glory.

It was in this era that the Walloons became fixed in those habits of industry, amounting almost to a passion, for which they are proverbial and which no wars or desolations have been able to quench. In all the centuries, these traits have stood them in good stead. In every case, after foreign invasions, the invincible industry of ceaselessly busy men and of their helpmates, the women, have conquered their conquerors.

Long afterwards, when in America, it was the inherited habits of their descendants, in both love of work and the saving of time, that made the wilderness so soon to blossom and the soil so quickly to laugh with new flowers and luscious fruits. In the assemblage of those qualities that make the best type of American, not one strain of humanity has excelled the Huguenot Walloon.

CHAPTER V

THE GLORIOUS BURGUNDIAN ERA

THE era of the Dukes of Burgundy (1384–1476), rulers of the Netherlands, was one of unification, during which the people of the Low Countries attained national consciousness. It was the era also of the rise of the communes and of the growth of cities.

Leaving out the history of Flanders, or the North, and confining our view chiefly to the South, we note the general commercial prosperity of this era; especially since, in the long run, it was industrialism and commerce which, more than any other factors in the case, broke up feudalism — their own particular form of which, the Burgundian nobles fondly hoped would last forever.

In actual fact, the dukes, counts, and feudal barons had made themselves poor in the Crusades, while the merchants and artisans increased in wealth. They bought from the castle lords both land and privileges, which were secured by being written down in charters. The commoners were thus able to have towns and cities, to build walls around them, and to choose their own rulers and soldiers, and so to possess rights which only at their peril the lords of the land might attempt to seize, annul, or dare to trespass upon. In time, there were in the Low

Countries over two hundred of what were, in effect, city republics.

Yet during this time, the wealthy Netherlands were coveted by the potentates of Germany and France, whether of petty degree or of grand pretensions, while there were also many bloody battles between lords and vassals, between dukes and mechanics, besides frequent struggles, not racial, but economic, within the borders of Belgic Land. Victory was at times on one side and again on the other. On a field of carnage and corpses, as at Courtrai, in 1302, one could collect hundreds of pairs of golden spurs and suits of armor of French knights. On another, as at Roosebeke, in 1382, there were counted thousands of pikestaffs and dead men in common clothes.

The communes or democratic communities arose from men determined to be free, yet their basis was economic, and both the ideals and the experience gained through centuries by certain stable representative governments were lacking. For permanent prosperity, the staple article they needed was wool. This product of the sheep was raised chiefly in England, where were millions of lambs, rams, and ewes, but very few weavers, and most of these had come from across the English Channel. Every year the wool fleet left the English seaports to carry over the fleeces and bags of the fiber which, transformed by intelligence, made warmth for the body and beauty to the eye.

There was no true national consciousness among

the Netherlanders until the time of the Burgundians, who welded the seventeen provinces into one commonwealth. Besides this, these dukes were in one way the educators of Europe. They introduced refined manners and improved society in all the courts of Europe. Instead of the nobles spending their time chiefly in jousts, or rough exercises, or hunting the wild boar and deer in the forests — which then covered the land from the Rhine to the ocean — or carousing in their castles, the feudal lords were summoned to the court to attend upon their overlord, the Duke. They were thus brought near the cultivated ladies, the scholars, the poets and learned men. This was a sensible proceeding and wrought much good, for very few of the mediæval knights, who in war wore clothes of iron and leather and in peace liked rough outdoor life, could read or write.

Apart from their own ambition to govern with power and enjoy the wealth of the richest part of Europe, the purpose of the Burgundian dukes was to create a state that should be independent of either France or Germany — from which came frequent invasions, besides constant interferences. Some of the finest monuments in the Belgium of to-day tell of battles with, or victories over, French knights and German armies. Belgic Land has been for ages the cockpit or quarreling ground of the two races, Frankish and Teutonic, that seem to have chronic dislikes and animosities. Between their undying rivalries, Belgic Land, with a new sense of nationality, was to

stand, holding the balance of power, like the governor on a pair of scales. To be a "buffer state" means
to be a shock-absorber in a collision, or a cushion in
the concussion between two rivals, or the peaceable
victim between contending armies.

To the great scheme of the Dukes of Burgundy, in
unifying many fractions of sovereignty, there were
two obstacles, the northern industrial cities in
Flanders, like Ghent, and the great trading centers
like Antwerp. There were also, in the Walloon manufacturing city of Liège, independent and powerful
bishops, who ruled as lords of the land. It was
of these interior jealousies that King Louis XI of
France hoped to make use in attempting to checkmate the plan of Belgian unity. In rivalry and opposition, Charles the Bold (1433–77) tried to reës-
tablish the old ninth-century Kingdom of Lothair,
making all the border lands of western Europe into
one state.

Most of the Dukes of Burgundy were wise rulers,
but in the case of Charles the Bold, or the Bully, we
have an example of the kind of rulers feudalism is
apt to breed. This despot thought nothing of punish-
ing a revolt by reducing a town to ashes and then
hanging, shooting, or drowning its inhabitants by
the thousands. He well deserved his fate when he
tried the same game of brutality with the brave
Swiss. At Nancy, January 5, 1477, he was slain, and
his banners and the trophies picked up on the bat-
tle-field now hang in the museums of Switzerland,

while democracy in that mountain land, whose people assisted so largely to build up Pennsylvania, is safe to this day.

At Bruges, the tourist visits one of the most magnificent tombs in Europe. It is that of Charles the Bold and of his daughter Mary. In those days, beautiful girls, or even homely and stupid princesses, were pawns in the games of kings, who used lands and peoples as if they were nothing more than dominoes or pieces on a chessboard. To get a royal or princely girl for a wife, in this style, seems to us only another form of marriage by capture, in African fashion, or the sale of a woman for cows or cowrie shells. Yet this was the time "when knighthood was in flower."

Louis XI was eager and anxious to get the Princess Mary of Burgundy, only daughter of Charles the Bold. There was no love in the scheme, but only the gambler's hope of a winning game. Yet with all his craft and power, he failed miserably. So, to vent his spite and malice, he seized those territories of the dead Duke which lay in France. His excuse was that since Charles had no male heir, this landed property reverted to the French crown.

Much of this is told in the form of a story by Sir Walter Scott, in the romance of "Quentin Durward," which all should read. Yet even this great novelist makes the mistake of calling the men "Flemings" and making his hero appear to talk Dutch, when everything in the situation and even the speech

39 .

shows that they were Walloons. However, in the older English literature, "Flanders" usually meant all Belgic Land, and "the Low Countries" the whole of the seventeen provinces. Even now, "Holland" — the name of but one of the eleven provinces which compose the kingdom — is applied by some foreigners to the whole realm of the Netherlands.

It was towards the end of the Crusades, when the half-civilized Occident touched the more civilized Orient, that commerce and the guilds of craftsmen were developed. The Town Hall and the Bourse, or Exchange, for the merchants, and the walled cities had not yet appeared; but these, along with the guilds or companies of working-men, were to come later. These were portents and signs that feudalism, in both Church and State, which in most countries of Europe lasted five hundred years, or from about the ninth to the fourteenth century, was being broken up and was ready to pass away.

By the end of the Burgundian era Belgic Land had taken on a notable and attractive feature which differentiates the Netherlands from almost any part of Europe, except where the Walloon speech and genius prevail. It had become the home, by excellence, of the bells. In this region, beyond all others, was there literally "music in the air."

One flower, especially associated in point of time with the Burgundian era, but now a familiar sight in the eastern part of the United States, is the meadow ornament, which has a yellow disk with white petals. This our Teutonic ancestors named from the sun the day's eye, or daisy, and Chaucer "the emprise and flower of flowers all." It may be called the flower of the Walloons. At the marriage of Charles the Bold with Margaret of York, England, a nosegay of these Marguerite daisies was among the most conspicuous of the floral gifts and decorations.

CHAPTER VI

IN THE TIME OF CHARLES V

ONE of the surest proofs that the seventeen provinces were attaining unity is seen in what happened in the year 1477. The poor German prince Maximilian I, who inaugurated the line that was disgraced by summary execution in Mexico, in our time, was the Emperor then. He married Mary, daughter of Charles the Bold. He wedded her first according to legal, not ritual, church forms; for, in the "Old" Church, marriage is a sacrament. Being in a hurry, too — for she was rich and he needed the money — occupied with much business, and not having much cash on hand for the journey, he was joined to her legally by proxy. This was a common custom in the European marriage market, among mediæval rulers, as has been shown in "Belgium: The Land of Art." Later the great Spaniard, the Duke of Alva, served in the same way for his master, the much married Philip II of Spain, when officially espoused to Elizabeth of Valois.

When, in due season, Maximilian and Mary had been regularly married, with the final public ceremonies, the couple made their "joyous entry" into the cities of the Netherlands, and the groom took oath to "support the constitution" by respecting old charters and the new requirements. Thus, by transfer of authority through matrimony, the seventeen provinces came under the rule of the House of Austria. From this time forth, until the French Revolution, the southern Netherlands were more and more sacrificed to the interests of their masters, whether belonging to the Austrian or the Spanish branch of the Hapsburgs. It became like a game of shuttlecock and battledore; Belgic Land being the ball between the players, Spain and Austria, varied by the interpositions required by Dutch and British statecraft.

But before the time of the wedding of Mary and Maximilian, which was within fifteen years of the discovery of America, the Netherlanders resolved to be sure of good treatment by the foreigner. They knew that when once they were within his grip, he would squeeze from them, in the form of taxes, all the money he could possibly get, to squander in some one of those interminable wars which were ever likely to spring up. When the men of privilege wore iron clothes, and a sword was part of their costume, settled peace was always an improbability.

Already the burghers had learned that good government cost money and must be paid for, yet, also, their motto was "no taxation without consent." So they waited upon the Princess Mary and demanded that she summon what we might call a parliament of the provinces, that they, and not the alien ruler, should set the limit of taxation. She must grant what was then, considering the ruling ideas of the age in other countries, a constitution, which should limit the ruler's powers. The document, which she finally signed and which granted much power to her subjects, was called "The Great Privilege." It became a living political force, efficient and active for over a century. It paved the way for the Republic of the United Netherlands, in 1579; the English Commonwealth of 1649; and the American Constitution of 1787; for mankind, in its action, is governed less by theories than by successful precedents, and every precedent counts, while movement in one country affects the life of another.

The discovery of America had a vast influence upon the politics, governments, and trade systems of Europe. Among other upheavals and readjustments, it made Spain the most powerful among the states of Europe, besides relatively projecting westward England and the other countries facing the Atlantic.

When in 1500, Charles V, the grandson of Mary and Maximilian, was born in Ghent, the rejoicings of both Flemings and Walloons were great. People went wild with delight. They were happy that now a Burgundian prince was once more their ruler, for it brought back the memories of the great prosperity and brilliant renown of their native land in that era.

Of this sovereign the world expected much. When he entered cities, as contemporary documents and pictures show, popular joy reached the point of delirium. Besides being King of Spain and overlord of the rich Netherlands, he became, at the early age of twenty, Emperor of Germany. His opportunities measured up to his titles and position. Yet he turned out to be a lover of continual war and of carnal pleasures. He became prematurely old and died a glutton.

At first, Charles followed out the policy of his Burgundian predecessors, in attempting to make the Netherlands the dominant state in Europe — thus holding at bay the great powers of France and Germany, both of which were equally ambitious and aggressive. They were always ready to renew their quarrels, which had already lasted a thousand years, on Belgic soil.

Yet notwithstanding his vast possessions in the Old and New World, and his enormous resources, Charles failed and finally abdicated the throne in favor of his Spanish-born son, Philip II, who was one of the greatest bigots of all time. Charles died of over eating, in a monastery in Spain. It was under his rule that the great surgeon Vesalius, a Fleming, made a wonderful advance in science and humanity by amputating the limbs of soldiers wounded in battle.

Despite all his faults, Charles V did much to give form and cohesion to the Netherlands and to increase the spirit of national unity. One of his creative works was the Raad van Staté, or Council of State, the supreme court of the land. This institution after many vicissitudes is still in existence. The most imposing modern edifice in Belgium is the Palace of Justice, in Brussels, which is built on the old site of the castle of the counts of Brabant. The American doctrine of judicial supremacy and the Supreme Court of the United States have come to us by direct evolution from this creation of Charles V.

In the time of Charles V there were two hundred and twelve walled cities in the seventeen provinces, and most of these possessed written charters. Some of these were older than Magna Charta and were published, not in Latin, but in the language of the people, which all could read and understand. There were many defects in the constitution of the Dutch Republic; but our fathers, in 1787, though repudiating the Dutch constitution as a whole, profited by history and experience to note these defects and to make improvements; for, as Hamilton wrote, "Experience is the oracle of truth."

The bringing of new ideas, through what we call the Renaissance, or the New Birth of Learning, which preceded the Reformation, had deeply stirred men's minds, and given them a new world of thought. In this movement, learned men used not only their eyes, but the pen and the spade. They dug up, copied out, printed, and exhibited the wonderful treasures in literature and art of the Hebrews, Greeks, Romans, and Arabs. They found out that there had been and were civilizations greater than their own.

History is a resurrection. At first, most of the

knowledge of such great ancients as Plato and Aristotle was made known in Europe through Arabic translations. In a large sense, "the glory that was Greece, and the grandeur that was Rome" had been unknown before to mediæval Europeans. By the multitude they were hardly suspected to have ever existed. The popular stories of the past were fantastic to the last degree. To discover the originals was as the finding of the continent of America by the men who followed Columbus.

In the time of Charles V very few people knew what the Bible was, except as the priests told them, or they learned from pictures, statues, tapestry, carvings, and miracle plays. The stories told in the pulpit were more or less funny, and in time the Passion Play became a Punch and Judy show — Pontius Pilate being Punch, and his wife, with the legendary name of Judith, being Judy. A great many notions and symbols, such as feminine angels with wings, were borrowed from Buddhism. Except priests and monks, the majority of people were totally ignorant of the Bible and its contents, and most of the men at the altar knew very little.

It was like thirsty souls coming to a living spring of water to read the Greek classics and the New Testament.

Columbus got his ideas about land lying in the western part of the globe from Plato's writings, which came to mediæval Europe through the Arabic. When the Saracens — a word meaning Ori-

entals and a general name for Turks and Moslems —
captured Constantinople, the Greek scholars fled to
western Europe, bringing with them the New Testament. Then it was that learned men found out in
what the true Church consisted and where lay the
seat of authority. They discovered that in the first
Christian congregations there were no pope or
cardinals, and that bishops were only pastors of
churches, or "overseers," while kings and politicians
had nothing to do with the conscience. Yet Christianity in the eyes of the State Church was branded
as "heresy," just as was the Reformation later.
"Life grows by 'heresies.'"

Moreover it was found that anciently, in the days
of the apostles, the people elected their own officers.
What was most to be feared by kings was the rule of
the people, as in the time of Moses, and the early
Jewish republics. The ancient literature showed
that this was by elders, and that when God gave
kings to Israel, He did it in his wrath and He took
royalty away in his displeasure; because though
called "the Lord's anointed," many of the kings
were bad rulers and wicked in their lives. Some
prelates even objected to translating the Bible into
the people's language, lest men should learn how to
swear worse than before.

It often happens that there are men born into the
world who are not blind with the eyes set in their
heads, but are utterly obtuse as to what is going on in
men's minds. Charles V was one of the most blinded,

48

partly because his chief business was that of a soldier and therefore he was interested chiefly in war. Yet he knew little and could comprehend less of the great movement of mind that was to create a new world of thought, worship, habits, and customs, and to renew society. Men had got hold of the original documents of Christianity. Reading these they found out how different was the primitive Church from the great corporation in Italy, which ruled men's consciences.

Erasmus, the Netherlands scholar, collected over three hundred ancient manuscripts and made a new translation from the Greek into elegant Latin. From this "received text" — the basis of our "King James Version" — translations of the New Testament were made into nearly every language in Europe. To-day, over twelve thousand manuscripts have been made use of by critics and scholars, and the Revised Version — the terror alike of ignorant "evangelists," reactionaries, and prelates, of both the Roman and the Reformed obedience — brings the record of the Church nearer to reality.

In the Netherlands, printing was free; which was not then the case in England. Before the English Bible was printed in England over a score of editions of the Bible, or parts of the Bible, had been published among the Flemings and Walloons in the Netherlands. One can go into the Plantin Museum in Antwerp to-day and see a printing office of the old time.

THE STORY OF THE WALLOONS

Yet even before 1453 and the exodus of the Greek scholars westward, the forces were gathering that were to bring in a new world of thought, of society, and of economics. It would take pages to catalogue all the elements in the dynamic that precipitated the Reformation, or to tell of the events and men and books that led up to it. Yet in the Netherlands, as in every instance before and in every case since, the Walloons were foremost in the great awakening of the sixteenth century.

"Light from the east!" A new world of joy was dawning.

The oncoming of the Reformation spoiled the colossal imperialistic schemes of which Charles V dreamed, and in the attempts to execute which, he dealt with human life as a player with tenpins. His Spanish son, Philip, came into the Netherlands unable to talk the speech either of Walloon or of Fleming, and only to make up his mind to murder thousands of human beings, in the name of God and the Church. Yet the spider in the Escurial, even while spinning his web of destruction, found in William of Orange the wasp that destroyed the spider's offspring; while on the day that Alva's "blackbeards" arrived on Belgian soil to do their work of death, there was born in Antwerp a baby boy, William Usselinx, who was destined not only to bring to naught the plans of Alva, but to father the West India Company of the Dutch Republic and inaugurate the colonization of Distinctive America.

CHAPTER VII

THE DEATHLESS BOOK

THE literature of the Bible is one of the most dangerous of elements to be feared by the opponents of
ordered freedom, whether in Church or State. This
is proved by that revolt against feudalism, whether
political or ecclesiastical, which broke out all over
western Europe, when the ancient literature of the
Hebrews and early Christians was put into the languages of modern nations. Those plain people, cari-
catured under the name of Anabaptists, did not
know enough to make out of Jesus what the men
who wore crowns and miters, or academic gowns and
caps, saw in Him, and they tried to reform society in
root and branch. Men of conscience holding Anabaptist ideas were quickly found in many countries
and especially in the Walloon provinces. Without
being met by argument or reason, they were burned,
drowned, and slaughtered as wolves or poisonous
vermin. In Belgic Land, both the Reformed and the
Romanists tried to exterminate the Anabaptists, so
called, by fire, burial alive, or the gallows.

Guido de Bray, the Walloon hero, was one of the
few who honestly tried to understand, while strenuously opposing them. His chief motive was to clear
those of the Reformed faith from false charges.
Probably the ablest intellectual argument written

against the Anabaptists, exposing their defects, was from his pen.

The Anabaptists ushered in the modern world. They were like those in the Orient, the once despised searchers into the secrets of Western science and freedom, who in Japan, China, and India suffered death for "introducing novelties" and "holding evil opinions" (Christianity). Both were pioneers who led the nations that have marched forward, making progress over the bloody tracks of the martyrs. To be put to death for conscience' sake means first the sowing of seed by the victims for larger world harvests. One of these victims taught the true philosophy when, flinching not from the gibbet, He himself dared to be the file-leader of the world's salvation and "endured the cross, despising the shame."

No attempt is here made to tell in detail of the "re-baptizers," upon whom the crimes of Münster are absurdly charged. No full account of these "pariahs of history" has ever been attempted, though the late Dr. J. G. de Hoop Scheffer wrote of those in the Netherlands and his work was crowned as genuine history by bodies of learned and judicial men. Under Menno Simons they were shepherded, and the Mennonites are perhaps their nearest representatives to-day. The first persons in England to receive Christian baptism, not as unconscious infants, or unreasoning children, but as adults with full mental powers, were Mennonites.[1]

[1] *History of the Free Churchmen* [Brownists, Pilgrim Fathers, and

THE DEATHLESS BOOK

These people were especially opposed to human slavery. It is a fact of history that we Americans received by direct inheritance our freedom, not from the "churches," then so-called, but from the "sects," which kings and prelates banned.

In the eyes of royalty and prelacy, the "damnable error" of the Anabaptists was that they believed in progress. They would change the existing order of things, which kept scepter and crozier, with their honors and revenues, in the hands of those who already held them. Down at the bottom, beneath all outward demonstrations, sometimes grotesque, the alleged heresy was a desire to change what, it was claimed, had been ordained of God and fixed since creation. It was not only "scoffers, walking after their own lusts," who said "since the fathers fell asleep all things continue as they were from the beginning of the creation"; but all orthodoxy, from the chair of St. Peter to the unlettered peasant, held that the order of the world, society, and the Church as then ruled, was fixed, and that to disturb it was worse than breaking the commandments.

The modern ideas of progress, now part of our vital breath, which we inhale when on our birth-beds, was utterly unknown. An individual might have visions, but the Church as a mass was crystallized. Even at the Reformation, there was surprisingly little change of dogma, and, with the orthodox, no at-

Baptists], by J. G. de Hoop Scheffer; W. E. Griffis, Editor. Ithaca, New York, 1922. Andrus and Church.

tempt to apply the new thought to social order. The pagan philosophers, Christian fathers, "the Holy Church throughout all the world," many Reformers, one and all, taught the fixity of things, which to disturb, or even challenge, was a crime. The earth, and even the universe, was as a cabinet, elaborately constructed and fitted together, but never to be touched for alteration; for change would mean destruction. Social reform would spoil honors, revenue, office, and power, and wither ambition. All truth was a "deposit" in care of the holy centralized Church, to be held as a sacred trust, never to be added to or diminished. It was already full day and no new sunshine, no fresh sunlight was to break out of the Bible, or the Consistory, or the Orient. All things were to continue as they were until the *Dies Iræ:*

> "That Day of Wrath, that awful day
> When man to judgment wakes from clay,"

and the elements were to "melt with fervent heat."

The Brethren believed differently. After they had digested the results of the Renaissance, or New Birth of Learning, as far as they could assimilate what they had learned, they got hold of the Bible. This was like adding a blast to the furnace, or wind to a prairie fire. It swept over Europe. It was a time of exhaustion, and the common people, after endless wars and distress from industrial oppression, were intoxicated with expected freedom. Liberty turned into license and some disturbances resulted.

THE DEATHLESS BOOK

Yet with how little wisdom was the world governed! The authorities in Church and State, instead of seeking the cause and laying the axe at the root of the trouble, could see only the outward and destructive phases. They were too blind, too hardened in routine to discern the creative energy inherent in the movement. In the score of crimes alleged against the Anabaptists, the capital charge was that they stood for progress. They wanted to change things. That meant heresy. The Church had built itself upon the motto of Tertullian, given in the third century: "A rule of faith changeless and incapable of reformation." So fire, flood, the gallows, and the sword were invoked for the suppression of these militant reformers.

Nevertheless to-day church edifices stand on the old ash heaps of human fuel, and "the sects" can look back on victories which "the Church" claims as her own. The time did indeed come when not only the Church, but the Reformers needed reforming. So the Quakers, the Methodists, the Mennonites, and other contestants for the excellency of the knowledge of the Master, entered the race. In the perspective of years and the vision of to-day, can any show a better record than that of the Friends?

Whether as friend, critic, or enemy we judge State and Church persons, events, or movements, we should not fail to recognize the good in all and note what has been done by them. My own ideas about the Anabaptists were given in "The New

55

World" for December, 1895, after visits to their churches and historic places in the Netherlands, interviews with their people there and in our country, and some study of their history and beliefs. The quotation here made seems more than ever true and pertinent, after the great military upheaval, from 1914 to 1918, in which the failure of the Sword to bring order in the world was shown and when the taunt of the smug churchman, "He saved others, himself he cannot save," may have a suggestion of another and the right way. The Anabaptists made at least the attempt to walk in the Christ's path.

Interpreting then the movement called "Anabaptist," which began as soon as the Bible was widely read in the vernaculars of Europe, in the light of to-day, when over the fairest parts of the earth kings are becoming phantoms and political bishops shadows, when republics are common and the Constitution of the United States, an Anabaptist document, is over one hundred years old, we find these to be the fundamental doctrines of the people [the Anabaptists] who tried to take Jesus Christ seriously.

1. Separation of Church and State.
2. No official meddling with the conscience.
3. No persecution on account of religion.
4. Every man free to worship God according to the dictates of his own conscience.
5. No damnation of infants.
6. The salvation of the God-seeking heathen.
7. The priesthood of all believers.
8. All the commands of Christ binding.
9. Honest translations of the Bible.
10. The Bible in the hands of the people.

THE DEATHLESS BOOK

11. The Written Word to be honored, but not worshiped.
12. The Holy Spirit to be constantly sought for aid and guidance.
13. Self-governing churches, with the rights and powers of the congregation, as set forth in the New Testament.
14. The validity of congregational ordination of pastors and teachers, who were not necessarily to be a distinct class.
15. Congregational singing. (The Anabaptists made and sang some of the very first modern evangelical hymns.)
16. Home and foreign missions. (By the very terms of their church membership, they were missionaries; they understood and practiced "beginning at Jerusalem.")
17. Social and political, as well as ecclesiastical reconstruction.
18. The reform of penology and of prisons. (Most of them held to abolition of the death-penalty and to the root-idea of the indeterminate sentence, both here and hereafter.)
19. No human slavery or serfdom, but the equality of all men.
20. The education of women and the equalization of the sexes, especially in religious life and privilege.

In a word, unless we have misread their own confessions and the creeds which they were driven to formulate, and unless we mistake the voices heard out of the dungeon, rack, and fire, the above articles, in outline, constituted the faith of the people whom the magistrates and churchmen of the sixteenth century — excepting only William the Silent and the Dutch Republic — felt it necessary to exterminate. In Anabaptist confessions, oral and verbal, we discover the seed-bed of the great truths now held by us as most precious. The form in which the Brethren tried to realize their vision seemed, three centuries and a half ago, as destructive to the institutions then existing as Christ's real teachings actually are to the selfish and ambitious holders of wealth and power to-day.

CHAPTER VIII

WHERE AND WHEN BEGAN THE REFORMATION?

THE Huguenot Walloon is the child of the Reformation.

If we must insist upon setting a date, or naming a place for the visible beginning of that very complex movement called the Reformation, we may as well look to Paris, and find the man, who spoke in the French language, which the Walloons not only talked but read. The word "Protestant" refers to an event in Germany, while the term "Catholic" has been corrupted from its original meaning. A far better term, descriptive of Christianity, when stripped of its accretions and deformities, is the word "Reformed," while the phrase in the creed "The Holy Christian Church" is one untainted with the notions of sect, locality, or monopoly.

It was the Bible, and not any "sect" or "church," that turned the old world upside down and ushered in a new and better one. It was ancient literature that kept burning the torch and lesson of ordered freedom which we enjoy to-day. It was as much through music and song, as by sermon, or reading, or preaching, that the spark of the new fire became a revolutionary conflagration. The pathway for the Calvinistic or Reformed phase of the faith — as depicted in the sculptures of the Monument of the

Reformation in Geneva and unveiled in our decade
— was made clear.

If music be conceived of as a universal language, in
its appeal to the emotions, then also in the Netherlands we may discern the home of modern music and
the original of its notation. Among other eminent
and creative musicians was Josquin des Pres, or
Depres (1450–1521); the foremost composer of his
age, who developed counterpoint. He won even the
praise of Luther, and he certainly prepared the way
for the Reformation, by adapting musical themes to
the words of the piece. His journey to Rome marks
the transfer of the musical art from Gallo-Belgium,
its birthplace, to Italy; which for two centuries there-
after was the center of the musical world.

Reformed Christianity in France was not of foreign origin. It grew up on the soil. Years before
Luther, Calvin, or Zwingli, France was astir with
thought and there was a great outburst of literary
activity following upon the new learning. In the
university of Paris, one of the oldest and greatest in
Europe, the theological division was the Sorbonne.
In a true university, theology — which is the adjustment of what man believes with what he knows — is
studied as one of the sciences. More and more, in
America, our purely sectarian schools of divinity
receive less support and are being affiliated with
universities.

When popes, emperors, cardinals, and kings
looked at the "sects" of free churchmen which arose

THE GREAT MONUMENT OF THE (CALVINISTIC) REFORMATION AT GENEVA (1918)

from the study of the Bible, they were both surprised and amused at the idea of these having any power, or even any future. They called the Reformed the "Pretended Religion."

The idea that from a literature alone, without a thousand years of organization, force, and economic values behind it, there could issue any permanent potency for the making of new men and a new society, was regarded by prelates as rather a good joke.

The history of the last four hundred years shows that these "sects" which had most to do with making the Dutch Republic, the English Commonwealth, and the United States of America, had more power than the popes, emperors, and kings, dynasties and conquerors, that have come and gone.

There was a professor in the Paris University, born in 1496 and bearing a name that is common in our telephone directories, La Febre, or Lefevre, a Doctor of the Sorbonne. He was what is called, even yet, a "good Catholic." Studying the Bible, he found in it much wonderful truth and many fresh ideas — as all will who make themselves familiar with the old writings of deep thinkers, whether in "the classics" or "Holy Writ." Mr. Gladstone and the Pope alike recommended the study of ancient theology to freshen the brain. Such study unshackles the mind.

Lefevre introduced the study of this wonderful literature as a new science — or one old enough to seem new — and gave lectures upon what he had

read. The lords and ladies of the Court attended
and were delighted. The King's sister, Margaret of
Valois, a highly cultivated woman, with many of
the nobles, was charmed and became an adherent.
Work went on and ideas spread. Even bishops co-
labored with Farel, the Swiss Reformer, whom we
may call the spiritual father of Calvin. It was he
who told the King of France that the Huguenot
anvil would wear out all hammers that strike it.

France had three other teachers, who were in
Paris at one and the same time, Calvin, Rabelais,
and Loyola. The first was the champion of freedom
and democracy in the Church and of our public
schools. Our great historian Bancroft fitly calls Calvin "the father of popular education, the inventor
of the system of free schools."

Rabelais destroyed respect for sacred things and
good government. Yet to his influence, the great
Belgian prose epic "The Legend of the Glorious
Adventures of Tyl Ulenspiegel," which Charles de
Coster put in modern form, owes its existence.

Loyola instituted the order of the Jesuits, which
were later driven out of nearly every country in
Europe.

"It was a time," Guizot tells us, "when two con-
trary winds were blowing over Europe . . . one car-
rying skepticism and licentiousness, while the other
breathed only Christian faith and the severest morality."

France made her choice, with the result that the

WHERE THE REFORMATION BEGAN

French became great in everything but religion, morality, and self-government. The aristocratic in France found the Bible religion too severe. Instead of Calvinism, with its high and pure virtue and serious temper, the French rulers chose rather to follow tradition, frivolous skepticism, and reactionary fanaticism — which issued in as cruel persecutions as ever were known to Iroquois, Apaches, or Pawnees. From the seed sown by her accepted teachers she reaped the harvest of the Revolution of 1793.

The same methods as those used in war in Asia and in Africa were employed in France and Spain to stamp out the New Religion, as it was called. Steeped in the ideas of feudalism, men in Church and State imagined that truth was like wood and could be burned to ashes by fire. Dr. Guillot was not yet born, and the sheep-killing machine, which he invented and which was named after him, was not yet in use for human beings; but the fire, the sword, the scourge, and the red-hot iron were at hand. The decapitating machine, that made Paris a slaughter house, came later.

The king, Henry IV, who was at first delighted with the old truths so freshly presented, changed his mind. Surrounded as he was by priests and monks, he began to think it dangerous when such a book got among the common people. Priestcraft, in every land and age, is always in terror of too much general education among the people. The New Testament, when translated into French, which every one

THE STORY OF THE WALLOONS

could read, meant what the Great Democrat and Lover of the People had said, "The truth shall make you free." In the older Testament, they found that a large part of it consisted of the history of slaves, who had escaped from tyrant kings and formed republics and chosen their own rulers, and that this early history was followed by good laws and songs of deliverance. That is what the Old Testament consists of — Law, History, Poetry, and Prophecy, or, in the Hebrew Bible, of Law, Prophecy, and Literature.

At once the French monarch and court, kingcraft and priestcraft, saw the danger of letting the people know the Bible record, which showed that kings and the so-called saints were sinners like common people.

So "the King's religion" prevailed by the power of the sword, the fagot, and the dragoons. These hunted out Christians, as bloodhounds were used to track out slaves, and they did their work thoroughly. Like a lioness devouring her cub, France, having tasted the blood of her own children, was roused to a fury of hate, and sent them into exile. Thus she helped to enrich other countries, to colonize America, and to make herself poorer. When at last she had a revolution, which swept away feudal and royal ideas, while so changing the method of holding property as to become the country with the greatest number of landowners, her manner of doing it, in frightfulness, startled the world. The French Revolution set a red blotch on the pages of history, with reactions toward two eras of Napoleonism. Emissaries in President Washington's time attempted to infect America with French notions and methods of revolution; but the teachings of Calvin, Luther, Zwingli, as much as the Anglo-Saxon inheritances and the firmness and vision of Washington, saved us from "the red fool fury of the Seine," giving us orderly evolution, instead of a revolution that broke with the past.

In French history the Huguenots became a powerful political party, as well as an ecclesiastical body of believers, whose activities need not concern us here, except so far as to differentiate clearly the ethnic relations of the two Christian communities, Belgic Walloon and French Huguenot, that held to the same form of faith and spoke the same language. Both helped in the one object and enterprise of becoming inhabitants of those United Colonies, to which, on the 9th of September, 1776, by the Continental Congress, was given the name of "The United States."

The true origin of the term Huguenot is not certainly known. It has been sought to be derived from a small coin, minted in France about 1560; from the German word, eidengenossen, meaning men banded or confederated; from the saint, Hugo; from Huss-guenons, Huguenons, or apes of John Huss; from the Flemish Heghenen, meaning precisian or Puritan; or even from a mispronunciation of the old Greek term for gnostic or heretic. It is most probable that the English form of the word came in from the Low Countries, where "Huguenoot" referred to one in the household of the [Reformed] faith. Both "Walloon" and "Huguenot" follow the same analogy of form, spelling, and pronunciation, though the latter was shortened to its present form.

Whatever be the origin of the term "Huguenot," or of Reformed Christianity in France, neither was of foreign origin. Both grew up out of the soil, as naturally as a violet or a lily, and the perfume of the lives of the converts was like that of the flower gardens. The term as that of a distinct party was not applied until about 1560, the partisans of Henry IV being so called.

Any fixed system, by which men make money, get their living, or gain revenue, honor, ease or privilege, is hard to change. Those who try to reform it are considered dangerous enemies to society, and as not only heretics, but even traitors. Greed, ambition, love of pleasure and comfort may be rooted in any religion, so miscalled. It is so much more easy to use force, instead of brains or argument. So in France, Reformed Christianity was put down by cavalry, infantry, and artillery, by massacre and fire, and the Huguenots were cast out. Yet the process was like shoveling gold into other lands and thus mightily enriching England, the Dutch Republic, Denmark, Sweden, Russia, Germany, Switzerland, the two Americas, and South Africa. Nevertheless, Christianity was itself a heresy banned by the Church and therefore under political persecution, wherever Church and State were united. "The world grows by heresy."

In Belgic Land, the Walloons were and are always ready for new ideas, even though they do not hold to them or persevere as tenaciously as do the Flemings. Being so near France, the fires of faith were easily kindled among them. The Walloons exercising their minds, tens of thousands of them quickly became Huguenots in their church life. The province of Hainault and the city of Valenciennes were the *foci* of their activities. We must not forget that some of the richest cities now in northeastern France were formerly Belgic and Walloon.

Walloons and French love music and song. In 1540, in Paris, Clement Marot, professor of Hebrew at the Sorbonne, who has already been noticed, wishing to improve the public taste, translated into French verse some twenty — and still later, thirty of the psalms. The words, fitly chosen, were full of beauty and sweetness. The metre was in the style of the popular ballads, which everybody could sing and the melodies were "catchy"; for here was a case of "immortal music married to immortal words." Marot built his "miracle of song" on the foundations laid by Depres. Soon the ladies and gentlemen at Court were singing Holy Scripture in verse.

Then the fashion spread rapidly to all classes. Without knowing or intending it, Marot gave a

mighty impulse to the gospel and the religion of the
apostles' days. In the Swiss Republic, the Frenchmen, Calvin and Beza, saw at once the power of music and song, which even boys and girls enjoyed.
They realized that congregational singing, as if on
wings, would make the gospel fly into many lands.
So Beza translated and versified a hundred more of
the Hebrew psalms, making a hymnbook for the
whole body of Huguenot churches. These, in many
editions, were bound up with the Bible.

The joy and delight of the popular singing of holy
thoughts and words spread like a prairie fire over all
Europe. Instead of the churches having only old
Latin choral music, as sung by a *few*, the glad mes-
sages from Holy Writ were heard in song by hundreds of congregations. In tens of thousands of
homes, hearts and voices were joined to make better
life and manners and love of the beautiful. At first
and for some years, all Christians of every name
joined in psalm singing for mutual good. Later on,
Christians enjoyed a glorious hymnology, which
enriched life in church and home.

In the songs and music of Marot, which are the
same as are still sung in the Huguenot churches
throughout the world to-day, the undying fire of the
Hebrew lyrics was enkindled anew. They very early
resounded in the Walloon homes in New Netherland
and New York. When after 1685 this Middle Region of toleration began to be peopled by Huguenots
from France, Marot's psalms were heard in place of

chimes or carillons. The worshipers, on foot or in ve-
hicles, journeying every Saturday for divine service,
from New Rochelle to the Marketfield Street church
on Manhattan, compassed the long distance from
New Rochelle with these songs of joy and deliverance.

The new life of Europe, in the Reformation, began in France and Belgic Land when music was in its
renaissance with song, organ, and carillon; for even
the chimes in the belfries rang out Marot's psalms.
In Germany, the Reformation, starting in the time
of the new invention, or importation, of movable
types, proceeded more by printing presses, ink, and
types. Two hundred thousand Bibles are said to
have been produced within a decade.

By contrast in the air, by voice and in the heart,
it was melody that rolled out from the Huguenots
wherever found. French music is infused with passion, German with intellect, Italian with melody.
This grand passion in the soul issued to the making
in time of a new France, which, in our day, after
many reverses and afflictions, has come to the Huguenot position — liberty of conscience and of private judgment, free public schools, general education, and a republicanism tending to democracy; in
a word, to the ideas of Calvin, one of the most illustrious of the many illustrious sons of France.

In the Netherlands, the land's Lord Paramount
was that same Philip II, who " promoted the colonization of America " in two ways: first by sending,

in 1565, a naval expedition with twenty-five hundred men, to murder the French Huguenots in Florida and to destroy their settlement; and, in the second place, by depopulating as far as he was able the richest part of his dominions and of Europe, the Netherlands. "In 1566, he wrote to his ambassador at the Holy See, to tell the pope, that if he found himself obliged to use force it would 'involve the utter destruction of this country'! But he added that he would resolve on that rather than 'be in thought or will a lord of heretics.'" A few years later, unable either to forget or to learn anything, he dispatched for the conquest of England another naval expedition, pompously named the Invincible Armada, — loaded with bilboes and shackles — and all done in the name of Christ and of the saints.

After such exhibitions of insanity in rulers, one need not wonder at the rise of a new kind of state, such as the American Commonwealth, from which kings and thrones and the powers of united Church and State were abolished.

Philip II had only royal and autocratic ideas and thus he reasoned: was not his army not only the finest in Europe, the first to be armed wholly with muskets, and were not the two thousand women (of the wrong kind) sent too in the name of the Holy Father in Rome and the Holy Mother Church, to sally forth as Crusaders to convert or kill? Alva would attend to both orthodoxy and economics — enforce Christ's blessed gospel and also lay a tax of the tenth penny. How could God allow failure to such a beneficent policy? Yet somehow the Netherlanders could not and would not agree to this. So they were heretics.

The world of to-day rejoices in a more hopeful Spain and a more spiritual papacy for the blessing of mankind.

CHAPTER IX

THE WALLOON HERO: GUIDO DE BRAY

THE prelates soon discovered that the new music, and especially the words of the Hebrew lyrics put into French, were not favorable to the centralized government of the corporation at Rome. Under influence of the powers ruling supreme in that city and region, the Old Church people gave up congregational singing, and let the Reformed children of faith and praise have the new songs all to themselves.

This was like "giving wings to a tiger." It put into the hands of Calvin and the Geneva reformers, who were passionate lovers of beauty and true art, a tremendous weapon of defense and an instrument of propagation, which is powerful even to this day. With vocal music and popular song, the good news of God flew, as on wings to millions, whose only idea of what the Bible was had been derived from the mass and ritual — told in Latin, a dead language. Now, with the Bible, the literature of power, put into a tongue which the people could understand, with song and psalm on their lips also, not only in the church, but in the home, at work, and in play, the morning of a long day of general happiness broke brightly. In all the human story none has laid a

broader or firmer basis for "the durable satisfac-
tions of life," or of enduring joy and power, than the
Puritan — the true son of truth, and not his coun-
terfeit, the hypocrite.

Yet in this new pleasure, there was something else
than sensuous and intellectual enjoyment. It led to
better standards of life, purer and more exalted. It
helped to banish the low, vulgar songs of lust. Those
who have read of the cult of St. Goliard and the vile
abuse made of "music, heavenly maid" by male
singers who had good voices, but bad characters,
and the moral devastation wrought by them, can understand the purifying and uplifting power of the
new music, on which floated divine and inspiring
thoughts.

Hence from the first, the Huguenots were noted
for the singular purity of their lives. Indeed, they
have ever been the salt which has preserved what is
best in the life of modern France, where conscience is
now free. Ethics and religion were vitally connected
and the one fed the other.

While in England and Scotland too many of the
Puritans cast away their organs and musical instru-
ments, the Netherlanders retained these to their
profit. Their congregational singing, thus improved,
had no superior in any land.

Nevertheless, after ascribing to music and song
their full part in the awakening of the Netherlanders
to reform in religion, we must not ignore other influences, deep, lasting, and long at work, in transform-

ing especially the Walloons. Seen in perspective the succession of vivifying ideas is almost unbroken.

During the onrushing centuries, from the time of the Verdun Compact, in 843 A.D., to the great Reformation, the twofold development of the Belgic people went on. In Flanders, civilization was more and more influenced by Germany, Flemish blood and speech being more akin to those in the Teutonic world. The southern or Walloon people were moulded by the fortunes and culture of the Gauls, the Gallo-Romans and the French.

During these centuries the work of the Church and the saints or missionaries was a noble one, for the whole country became more or less Christian. Roughly we may say that several civilizations, one after another, with their representatives, in speech, ideas, and dynasties, had come and gone. Under the Romans, Christianity made a beginning in softening rude manners and in every way improving the conditions of social and political life. The Romans introduced many good things, such as roads, farms, letters, writing, and architecture.

The Franks came out of the Northeast. They destroyed in large measure Roman civilization, but they built up another, different in form and spirit. Coming as pagans, they adopted Christianity. The Frankish Empire, under the Church and civilization, was rebuilt. There were still much cruelty and barbarism, but the teachers of religion strove "to bring charity, art, and culture into the world."

So we may say that as the pagan Celts had been civilized in the third century, so the pagan Franks were in the seventh.

Then out of the North, but nearer the pole and from the lands of the aurora borealis, Sweden, Norway, and Denmark — they were all "Danes" then — came the Normans, or Norsemen, in their keeled boats with dragon-prows, piloted by the ravens. Being one in their savagery, greed, traditions, and impulses to exploration, their expeditions were not at first strictly in the interests of science, or art, or religion. Yet they were partly Christianized and they too advanced Belgic civilization. Under them, some of the oldest names now among us, such as Baldwin and de Forest, had their origin. When they left the country, barbarism again triumphed over civilization, and the work of the Church had to be done over again with greater zeal and earnestness.

With the churches was ushered in the era of the bells and belfries, adding new features to the Belgic landscape and making of the Netherlands the Country of the Carillons. The first idea and purpose of the bells, when joined to the church edifice, was to warn off all imps, demons, and evil spirits. Later they were rung in storm, or at the hour of dusk to guide travelers to shelter.

During these centuries, from the ninth to the thirteenth, the Christian Church, in its various external forms, was the mother of art, while the sacred edifices, along with the castles and monasteries, be-

came the most characteristic features of the landscape, so far as this was affected by man. The influence of religion penetrated the family and beautified
the home. The lives of the good men and women in
the Church were models for imitation, and the baptis-
mal names of infants were borrowed as inspiring re-
membrancers. Even the leader of the Walloon settlement of 1624 in New York, Jesse de Forest, bore a
name which of old was Josse, that of a Belgian saint.

Some scholars — usually devoted followers of the
papacy — think that the thirteenth was the greatest
of all the centuries. In one view it was, for, beside
its great creations, the Italian monopoly of the religion of Europe west of Constantinople attained its
highest splendor in this time of the "Middle," or, as
some say, the "Dark" Ages; while others think these
were the "Ages of Faith." Then the Bible was
heard of only in a dead language, and few could read
or write. Celibacy had been made the rule for the
priests; that is, almost the entire body of educated
men were condemned to single life. Then the home
was degraded and centuries of intellectual sterility
followed. The celibate priest and knight, but not
the scholar or man of science, swayed the minds of
men. The thinker was feared, as if a child of the Evil
One. Only very few were able to form judgments
of their own.

Nevertheless there were always some who held to
the ideals of the Christ and his apostles and to the
simple norm of the Christian faith. To them Chris-

tianity was not a form of words, a set of symbols, or a method of government, but life — even the following of Him who "left us an example."

Among the Walloons in Belgic Land, for example, there was a continuous succession of teachers, who challenged the pretensions of the Roman corporation; such as Tanchelin, the Vaudois, Bulgares, Beguines, Lollards, Men of Intelligence, Brethren of the Free Spirit, the Bloemderdines, Brethren of the Common Lot, Hussites, Gondolfians, etc. All these paved the way for the Great Reformation.

The Waldenses of Italy, numbering thousands of Christians, held to the simple faith of the days of the apostles. When these were slaughtered, driven away, or exiled by the Dukes of Savoy, they found a champion in Cromwell the Protector, in Milton the poet, and in Leisler the American. Hundreds of these people came to America, settling on Staten Island and in other places.

It was during these centuries, after the fall of the Roman Empire, that feudalism became the established order of society and government and the framework of morals. Many nations passed through its long discipline.

Another feature of organic life in the Walloon churches, derived from France, was the model of government by means of pastor and elders, with deacons to minister in charitable affairs. This governing body was and is called the Consistory — with scriptural authority exceeding that claimed by the papal Senate, or cabinet. The Consistory is made up of the officers of the church gathered together. In the earlier congregations, all members of the church voted. This ordered, this well-regulated democracy was astounding to royalty and the prelates. Even to-day there is an almost antipodal difference among native Dutch writers, in the method and spirit of their treatment of the history of the Fatherland, according as they have lived within, or without, the atmosphere of Christian home life and the democracy of the Reformed Church.

How ready the Walloons always had been to accept, or at least be interested in new ideas, is seen in the welcome they gave to the various forms of truth at different times, as set forth by earnest preachers; so that the region of the southern or Walloon provinces was called by the name (which the Dutch Republic afterwards received), "The Land of Heresy."

It has been remarked by Hansen, the penetrating historian of "The Reformed Church in the Netherlands," that "the attachment of the people of the Netherlands [Republic] to Calvinism [or ecclesiastical democracy] is in great part to be accounted for by the influence of the Walloon congregations." It is certainly worth recalling that the vengeful reprisals against Spanish tyranny and the legal murders wrought by infuriated Protestants in the form of burning monks alive, were at the hands of the Flemings, and not the Walloons. Hansen adds the names of the four eminent preachers of the Reformed

GUIDO DE BRAY

doctrines, Guido de Bray, Henry Modet, Franciscus Junius, of Walloon, and Petrus d'Athenus, of Flemish origin.

The very names of these Walloon churches, organized as early as 1561, reveal their animus as being gentle and charitable. They were known among themselves by distinctive terms, in imitation of the societies of the rhetoricians, such as the Rose Tree, Rosebud, Vineyard, Sword, Lily, Palm Tree, Olive Tree, Wheat Sheaf, Violet, and Roosevelt, or Rose Field. Of their secret synods, in the years 1563, 1564, 1566, the last was the most important. In 1567, the murderous Spanish army was on the soil and Guido de Bray was made a martyr to "truth on the scaffold."

This lion-hearted hero was one of the greatest of the Walloons. He was not a fighter with swords or spears, he did not burn men alive, or wish to do so, but with pen and voice he fought the good fight of faith, for purity of life and for the original genuine gospel. Our Motley, the fascinating historian, scarcely more than mentions the name of Guy de Bres, or Guido de Bray, and utterly ignores his work. Yet the Belgic Confession of Faith, from his pen, is one of the noblest monuments of Walloon literature. What he did proved to be even greater in lasting results upon four nations, Holland, England, Germany, and the United States than that of some of Motley's heroes, who occupy many pages in that author's dramatic narrative. To-day the Reformer's great writing, "The Belgic Confession," is studied on all continents.

Guido de Bray, or Guy de Bres (Flemish and Walloon forms of the same name), born in 1640 at Mons, had more to do with the making of the Dutch Republic and the United States of America than many a more famous man. He was a champion of ordered freedom in Christ, of liberty under law, and of the right of the individual to interpret the Scriptures. At that time, whether right or wrong, the general impression about these Christians nicknamed Anabaptists was, that they were opposed, not only to all order and government, but to all decency. Certainly in Hainault, in a time of economic distress, these turbulent people committed great excesses, yet they never equaled orthodox churchmen in brutality. Because of this wrong impression, sedulously kept up by the priests, thousands of innocent persons, Bible Christians, who were horrified at the idea of being anarchists, or violators of law, either human or divine, were put to death. This was because, as a rule, most people, including especially political church rulers, led by Alva, the Spaniard, were only too slow to discriminate, provided they could kill, burn, or — what was often the chief motive in the case — confiscate property whether of Catholic or of Protestant. Millions of human beings, pure and righteous in God's sight, have been put to death through ignorance or suspicion, and of these Alva slew thousands.

GUIDO DE BRAY

It was the mission of Guido de Bray to clear the good name of true Christians from specific slanders. He wrote a book, a rare copy of which the writer of this work has examined. It was directed against the Anabaptists. The chief motive for his composing the Belgic Confession of Faith was for the purpose of clearing his fellow believers from false charges.

His next great aim was to unite all Christians of the Reformed faith in one body of love and mutual service, but not by means of fire, torture, infantry, cavalry, and artillery, such as Philip II employed, but in charity, and through preaching, teaching, and representative government. At Poitiers, once a bloody field of war, he penned the great confession. No greater battle was ever fought or victory won than was wrought through the Belgic Confession.

As a student, he became master of languages, especially those in which the Bible was written, the Hebrew and the Greek — the languages that are never dead, but are ever fresh, provoking new thought. These tongues possess the power of an endless life and will never die while humanity lives.

When this hero, as brave as any soldier that ever charged a battery, found himself surrounded by spies and informers and likely to be imprisoned, and thus lose his opportunity, he fled to England, where were already thousands of his fellow refugees. In London he met the reformers Bucer, John a Lasco, and others. Above all things the Anglican prelates

81

wished theirs to be considered "a true Reformed Church." The old edifice of the Austin Friars had been given by Edward VI of England to the Belgic and Dutch Pilgrim Fathers. It seems a paradox, but the oldest of the existing Reformed Dutch churches was gathered on English soil. To this day, the Netherlands people in London meet here for worship in the tongue of their fathers. In the crypt of Canterbury Cathedral, a Walloon church has worshiped since 1550.

Curiously enough, the Tudor and Stuart kings allowed foreign Non-conformists to have their own church order, ritual, and doctrines, even when they hunted down and drove out to other countries the Free Churchmen who were native Englishmen. Economic motives and ideas of expediency prevailed. These industrious craftsmen enriched the realm.

Returning from his first exile, Guido de Bray stayed for a while in Mons (or Malines) and then went into Switzerland, studying first at Lausanne, then at Geneva. Coming into contact with the greatest minds in Europe — those of John Calvin and Theodore Beza — he became more and more in love with freedom and law, and a Divine government, older than kings or thrones.

Later, at Frankfort, where was a great congregation of Huguenot Walloons, and where Jacob Leisler was born, he made appeal for "the churches of the Netherlands waiting under the cross," whose emblem was the lily among thorns. At this time, thousands of Walloons, ancestors of many of the best Americans of to-day, were in the Rhine valley.

The uprising for liberty in the Belgic Netherlands in 1567, as in 1830, began in the Walloon country. The cleaning out of the church edifices of idols and images had aroused the wrath of the Spanish monarch Philip II — the same who ordered the massacre of the Huguenots in Florida, thinking he would prevent the colonization of America, or the future United States, by men who believed in progress. A force of mercenaries was sent under Noircarmes to Valenciennes, where lived Guido de Bray, "the most pestilential preacher" in Spanish eyes.

The special offense of this ancient and beautiful city, founded by the Emperor Valentinian, was that its citizens had refused to have quartered on them a garrison of mercenaries in Spanish pay. When the citizens further claimed the privilege of free worship as a right, there arose a storm of fury in Madrid at the Escurial, and in Brussels, where the regent Margaret lived.

The story of siege and assault, after the cannon had knocked the city to pieces, on Palm Sunday, March 23, 1567, is brief. "The chimes, which during the siege had been playing Marot's psalms, happened that morning to be sounding forth from every belfry the twenty-second Psalm: 'My God, My God, why hast thou forsaken me?'" It was the carillon of crucifixion. After the orgy of slaughter by sword, the two leaders, Guido de Bray and Peregrine la

Grange, were arrested. From prison they were pushed off the ladder, even while speaking to the crowd, and swung in air. They died in the body, to live in the hearts of thousands who helped to make America.

In the origin and development of that era in the Netherlands, which the men of one obedience call the "Troubles" and those of the other "The War for Independence," the Walloon provinces were the first to revolt against the despotism of abused power in Church and State, the first to be stripped of their population by flight, and the first to be forced into reacceptance of the Spanish yoke.

In January, 1579, the nobles in Artois, Hainault, Cambrai, and Walloon Flanders formed the Union of Arras, which stipulated that their true aim was to preserve the papal religion and uphold the authority of the King of Spain. This action, which meant secession from the States-General, was done against the protests of that body, which insisted that it was first necessary to "expel the cruel tyrant and common enemy of all the Belgic race."

Nevertheless, a few patriots in the free Walloon cities continued the struggle for freedom of conscience and of resistance to the Spanish tyrant. The last local revolt in the Walloon provinces was led by Jean de Condé. From him and his brother Allard are descended most of the Condés and Candees in the United States. A descendant Jean, or John Condé, settled near Boston, Massachusetts, in 1639. The exodus from Belgic Land, begun in 1544, had continued with scarcely an interruption until 1585.

What were the facts underlying this Union of Arras, which virtually closes the story of the Huguenot Walloons in Belgic Land?

It was wholly the work of nobles and prelates, who dominated in a land from which the best people, or probably ninety per cent, had fled, leaving only a scanty population of peasants, who had little or nothing to say about the acts of their superiors. The final and formal reconciliation with Spain took place May 15, 1579, and for over two centuries Belgic Land became the private property of the Austrians and Spaniards, and "the cockpit of Europe."

In January of the year 1579, the seven northern provinces formed the Union of Utrecht. With "freedom of religion for all men" — within their homes and in their sacred edifices — with welcome and shelter given to people of every creed and clime, the brilliant career — not of "Holland," but of the Republic of the United Netherlands — began. Not only in its early years, especially from 1544 to 1570, but from England in 1605 and later, when James I persecuted Dissenters, and from Germany, from 1618 to 1648, the Republic received thousands of Walloon refugees, giving to the world an inspiring example of tolerance.

What kinds of people and varieties of humanity were left in the southern Netherlands, after the Union of Arras, was clearly discerned in that series of devastating campaigns called the Thirty Years' War, from 1616 to 1648. Few bodies of soldiery ever exceeded, in sheer brutality and mere wantonness of butchery and destruction, the Austrian army, which was composed largely of non-Huguenot Walloons, led by John Tzerclas Tilly. This man, born in Brabant, proved himself a diligent pupil of such masters of savage warfare as Alva and Requescens. Succeeding Wallenstein, he stormed Magdeburg, May 10, 1631. "The unheard-of atrocities which he allowed the Croats and Walloons of his army to perpetrate, on this occasion, have affixed to his otherwise high reputation a foul blot, uneffaced by all the cosmetics of his numerous apologists. . . . On May 14 he made a solemn entry into the city [and] attended the celebration of a Te Deum in the cathedral."

CHAPTER X

THE CHURCH UNDER THE CROSS

MANY are the emblems of divine grace and help to human character, and of "the faith once delivered to the saints" — whether as tried and purified in the fires of persecution, or stainless and white amid worldliness.

In one sense, even the catacombs of Rome are as an art gallery, rich in the treasures of early Christian thought and feeling. Yet after such crude realistic illustration, which was chiefly mural, Christianity emerged from the caves and dens of the earth, into the open sunlight, first of toleration and then of freedom. Then, out of Christian faith and feeling, grew a new set of symbols. The mediæval ages gave expression to inward emotions, in art on canvas, in sculpture, carving, mosaic, and adornment in gold and colors, while from architecture — mother and nurse of all the arts — was born the Gothic cathedral.

Some of these edifices of aspiration and hope rose into glory on wings of beauty. Others, well called "frozen music," sang a hallelujah chorus to the Creator. The church spire pointed men's thoughts to things higher than earth. Eternity seemed to take visible form to men's minds and "bring all heaven" before their eyes.

87

THE STORY OF THE WALLOONS

Europe was made beautiful, as never before, by Christian art, that far excelled in charm both the days of classic form and the splendors of Oriental decoration; for, while the spirit and even the masterpieces of genius in Babylon, Egypt, Greece, or Rome were pagan and earthly, the soul of Gothic architecture seemed to soar, like an eagle towards Heaven.

Yet still in the cerements of dogma and in the fetters of human authority, the individual soul, at its best, dwelt only in "dim religious light." Moreover, as a sinister inheritance from the Jews, those who claimed the monopoly of religion made this an engine of government. They not only preached intolerance as a duty, according to alleged divine command, but they reverted to the old methods of Joshua in Canaan and Samuel in Israel, until they outrivaled Mahomet and his methods of propagating the faith.

Instead of believing in the infallibility of holy persecutors, two of the founders of America, Roger Williams and William Penn, taught that "whoever is right, the persecutor is wrong."

When the radiance of the recovered Holy Scriptures, as in a new morning, broke over Europe, there was erected even a nobler edifice. Though not made with hands, it outshone in spiritual glory even the visible grandeurs of St. Peter's, or Rheims, or Amiens. Invisible to the eye of flesh and blood, it was a building of the Spirit, with the adornment of private interpretation and beautiful with self-government.

It incarnated the apostle's word, "Where the Spirit of the Lord is, there is liberty."

The believer's earthly home became even more lovely than the cathedral. After the manner of the primitive Christians, there arose the reading of the Bible, in the household and family worship, based on the priesthood of believers, as authorized in the New Testament. In church life, "the crowning fact, the Kingliest act of freedom . . . the freeman's vote," became law and custom. Even the common man could see that in moral grandeur, self-government excelled that from the stately chair of the bishop under "the antique bowed roof.", In his approach, as invited guest, to the "sacrament," or oath of allegiance, at the Lord's Supper, and in direct prayer to the King of kings and Lord of lords, Our Father in Heaven, the glory of a private Christian could make ridiculous the pomp of crowned emperors and ecclesiastics in miters and millinery.

The rights of the true church member, guaranteed by the fundamental law of the Founder, as laid down in the New Testament, emptied papal conclaves and the centralized power by the river Tiber of all meaning. The bulls of the papacy, the edicts of autocrats, the mandates of kings touched him not. In himself and in the congregation, the communion of saints, he had not only the best rule of life, in self-restraint, but also the surest safeguard of public order and progress. Sweeping away the symbols, he reached reality. Yet for him eternal vigilance was the price of liberty, while keeping the middle path between the libertine and the autocrat in religion.

By rejecting this reformed constitution of society and casting out those who adopted it, France and the Latin nations became great in many things, but not in the path of that ordered freedom and self-government, which is even now uplifting all the nations of the earth. France, in many ways the hero nation, had to postpone, for nearly three centuries, the possibility of a republic and stable government. The French Revolution was the reaction against centuries of repression of mind and body. In our day, France has confessed her mistake by giving equal freedom to all cults, rectifying the mistake of centuries, and accepting the Huguenot contention.

When driven from the old houses of worship in the Netherlands, the Belgic Christians went into the fields, where "hedge preaching" and psalm-singing were the rule. Their churches were not made of stone, decorated with art or graven by man's device, but were under the blue sky, where God "spread out the heavens like a tent to dwell in." Instead of buttressed walls, towers, and spires of stone, lifted up towards the empyrean and which under the chisel were made to blossom into beauty, they found within their own souls the "little sanctuary" promised of God through the prophet of individual right, Ezekiel, and confirmed by the Founder of their faith, even though but two or three might gather in his name. It was God, not the Church, nor its edifices, creeds, and ritual, that was, as they confessed, "the overflowing Fountain of all good."

So in place of imposing interiors, luxuriant with tracery and adornment that feasted the eye, they met on field and pasture to a richer feast for the soul. They heard the good news of God in their own tongue, and they sang the twenty-third, the ninetieth, and other psalms with a fervor born of their own souls' experience. Then, when they were driven, by pike and cannon, like sheep before the wolves, into foreign lands, or compelled to hide in caves and dens of the earth, there blossomed out of the garden of their souls rich flowers of thought, white lilies of devotion, and, in daily life, even the more luxuriant fruits of the spirit.

These we see revealed in the symbolism of language and art. Less sensuous, but more appealing to the spirit, was the new language that spoke to the eye. There was never any divorce between Puritanism and art, when that art was truth. The richest bloom of the Netherlands soul, in color and on canvas, was when the Republic and Calvinism were in their highest power. Rembrandt incarnated the truth of the Reformed Walloon, Fleming, and Dutch soul — the sublimation of Netherlands history.

No wonder that the chosen emblem of the persecuted Walloons was "the lily among thorns," for to their purity of life even enemies bore witness. In all lands and ages, whether he be Hebrew, Buddhist, or Christian, the lustful and selfish man is angered even

to fury, by the Puritan's holy life. Non-conformity
is as hateful to the sensual or to the slavish conform-
ist as to bigot, skeptic, or agnostic. Neither libertine nor prelate loves to see the self-governed freeman, who rules his passions, appetites, and beliefs.
Even in Buddhism — the religion of a fourth of the
human race — the conception of Amida, the man
who, having walked in the noble eightfold path of
virtue, has conquered himself, is one of the noblest.

Unchoked amid the thorns of sectarian hatred,
their own animal lusts, or the giddy pleasures of the
wanton and drunken, the white lily of Walloon faith
kept erect in heavenly purity, ever looking up to
God. Yet outwardly were the thorns, which lacer-
ated and with many, ended life.

This phase of the awful reality of persecution,
which hounded thousands to death, or, under allure-
ment, perverted the weak and discouraged, was
shadowed forth in their name as expressed in more
than one petition to their rulers for tolerance —
"The Churches of the Netherlands sitting (or waiting) under the cross," or, in brief, "The Church
under the Cross."

Even more personal for the individual, as well as
showing constant dependence upon the Holy Spirit,
was the symbol, wrought in gold, and worn on the
breast, or often hung between the heart and the armor. It represented the celestial Dove, emblem of
the descent of the Spirit, as seen of John at the bap-

tism of Jesus. This, the cross of Languedoc, in time became the special badge of the Huguenots. In their modern societies, their descendants keep alive, in grateful appreciation, the stirring memories of the past and cherish this symbol as a memorial of the martyrs. For even in our land, against any corporation that would again unite Church and State, and those enemies of religion who would break down all rule, order, boundaries, and safeguards, the citizen must ever be on his guard. "Eternal vigilance is the price of liberty."

The scattered groups of French-speaking Christians, especially in southern Belgic Land, were shepherded by two great organizers and preachers. One of these was Peregrine la Grange, who galloped on horseback to the great crowds in the fields, sometimes numbering twenty thousand, and signaling the commencement of divine service by firing a pistol in the air. This soldier of the cross, whose Christian name meant Pilgrim, was the Belgic Great Heart in undaunted courage and tireless energy. The other was Guido de Bray, who was more of a teacher. He not only roused the conscience and emotions of his audience, but he strengthened his followers to endure, by being able to give to every man a reason for the hope within him. Both became martyrs.

The first synods of the Walloon churches were held secretly April 26, July 24, and October 5, at Antwerp, in 1573.

THE STORY OF THE WALLOONS

What the dangers of the environment were is best
typified in the well-known picture of a real event,
painted by a modern Belgian artist. In Antwerp,
Franciscus Junius, afterwards professor in Leyden,
preached to his flock in a room on the walls of which
flickered the reflection of martyr fires in the square
below. Out doors, the Spanish Pilate and Caiaphas
worked together in planting the cross, and according
to the religion "established by law" men were burning Christians, their fellow believers, alive.

In the honor and shame of martyrdom the gay
city of Brussels excelled even Antwerp, and thence
a great exodus into Germany of young monks, students who had heard of Luther, their fellow Christian, began; for these seekers after truth were hungry for soul food. Hence also the barrier of fire,
reared to keep in the refugees! In the public square
of Belgium's City Beautiful, upon the two young
monks Esch and Voes was bestowed "the ruby
crown." Luther immortalized their names in deathless song.

In their chosen title itself, of "The Netherlands
churches which, sitting under the cross, are scattered
within and without the Netherlands," is a volume of
history; for even the first National Synods or general
gatherings, in council and for organization, were
held in the lands of exile. At Wesel, on the Rhine,
where then lived as pastor the father of New Netherland's first governor, Peter Minuit, the fugitives
gathered under the protection of the great Elector,

Frederick William, in 1568. On the second occasion,
they met at Emden, in the North. In this German
town, later under the protection of the Dutch Republic, the Dutch States-General kept a garrison for
many years, and there the seven-striped flag, which
guaranteed liberty of conscience, flew to the breeze.
Even to-day, with its dikes and quaint buildings
with their gable ends to the street, Emden has an
appearance more Hollandish than German.

Both of these synods were national or general, or
literally catholic. Local or provincial synods were
later held regularly in the provinces of the northern
Netherlands, which, in 1579, were united in the Republic. Those who have read, in either Dutch or
English, the romance by van Lennep, entitled "The
Abduction," will have a lively sense of the troubles
of a government in which the federal principle was
no stronger than under the American Articles of
Confederation.

In 1578, the grateful Walloons, with eloquent ora-
tions and fitting ceremonies, presented to the city of
Wesel two massive silver cups, decorated with the
figure of a pilgrim, that is, a Walloon, in token of the
hospitality enjoyed during more than thirty years.
Every American should see these memorials of gratitude.

In those days, in the very nature of the case, because of the terrible brute passions concealed under
the garb of religion, any moderate man, who stood
between the two fires and extremes and maintained

his poise, was apt to be suspected and slandered by both parties.

It was for this reason that such a great-minded patriot and Christian as William the Silent was so bitterly assailed by both partisans. The Spaniard called him a heretic, set a price on his head, and kept unsleeping assassins under pay to murder him, in which devilish enterprise they finally succeeded.

Yet hardly less bigoted were some of the ex-monks, who in turning their coats had become fanatical Calvinists, who burned alive their former brothers of the cell. These denounced the Father of his Country as a traitor and a papist. Nevertheless, the Silent One swerved not for a moment in his principle of "No interference with conscience by the magistrate." Besides William's personal motto, "Tranquil amid the waves," there was the necessity for action laid on him by the hereditary mandate, "I will maintain." In this frame of mind, head, and heart he lived and died. History now knows him as one of the heroes of all time. "He belongs to the ages." Not even English history, of which we who inherit its traditions are so proud, in all its long pageantry, has furnished one more worthy to be called a spiritual ancestor of the United States, than William the Silent.

Peter Dathenus, an ex-monk, was one of those wonderful men about whom the British encyclopædias are silent; for, as a rule, on topics of Netherlands world-interest these insular works of reference are

ALLEGORY REPRESENTING THE COMING OF THE PRINCE OF ORANGE

(From an engraving of 1572)

The Netherlands personified as Andromeda; the Prince as Perseus; Spain as the dragon. At the right are the provinces with their coats-of-arms

disgracefully defective. They ignore the men to whom the Netherlands biographical dictionaries give whole pages. Dathenus knew French, Dutch, and German. He had fled to the city of Frankfort — that oasis of freedom in a desert of persecution, which nourished so many of the makers of America. It was then crowded with refugees for conscience' sake from many lands, including some from England. Hundreds of these French-speaking people took German names. Here the future governor of New York, Jacob Leisler, was born, his father, so tradition states, being a Huguenot pastor.

Having sprung from the people, Dathenus knew their mother speech and their moulds of thought, so that he could both speak and write, as well as translate, in a way that appealed to their hearts and feelings. So, besides translating the Heidelberg Catechism into Dutch, he put Marot's version of the psalms into the same tongue. These were set to lively tunes and soon the whole Netherlands folk, old and young, were singing Bible words. Though a powerful preacher, Dathenus did more by song than by sermon; for it is ever true, as Herrick said, "A verse may find him who a sermon flies."

Dathenus most probably presided at the Wesel Synod of 1568, held the year after Alva and his Spaniards had invaded Belgic Land. Of the fifty-three names subscribed on the roll of attendance, that of Dathenus stands first. Then follow the names of Henry Modet, of Nyeveldt, whose psalms

97

in verse were in use in the Dutch church in London,
and of Philip Marnix de Aldegonde, whose name
is immortal in the history of the Republic.

It was decided at this Synod that Calvin's Geneva
Catechism in French, should be used by the Walloons, and the Heidelberg Catechism by the German
churches in the Republic. In the Church there were
to be four orders, those of minister, teacher, elder,
and deacon. Many copies of Calvin's Catechism, of
the service book of worship, and of French Bibles
printed in Geneva were brought to America by the
Walloon pioneers, and some are still to be found in
the homes of their descendants. Marot's and Dathenus' versions of the psalms have been sung by makers of the United States during several generations,
and still reëcho in hundreds of churches.

By the time that the first colony of Walloons was
ready in 1624 to start for America, their well-estab-
lished churches numbered over a hundred, twenty-
one then being in the Dutch Republic. All of these
were outside the southern or Spanish Netherlands,
though in the hiding places of dens and caves in the
home land a few groups of lovers of the Bible gathered secretly. There were Walloons at Delfshaven
when the Pilgrims sailed away, but no known church
was there of Huguenot faith, until 1686, or long afterwards.

In 1619 the great National Synod was held at
Dordrecht. At this "First Protestant Ecumenical
Council" — in describing which our Motley loses

his judicial balance as a historian and yields to subjective opinions and feelings — the Walloon churches were well represented, and many of their ablest and most eloquent pastors were present. Although there were one hundred and nineteen delegates from various countries, English, French, German, etc., there was no trouble in all being understood, during the fifty-seven sessions, for Latin was then the common speech of all educated men. Among those from England was the great Lancelot Andrewes, who gave the literary gloss to that masterpiece of translation, the English Bible; that is, the version of 1611.

It was a just criticism, made at the time, that the cast and Netherlands personnel of the Synod was largely political. Indeed, this Synod was called by government order. It was as much to decide an issue of administration, as to settle a dogma. In short, it was a stroke of policy and a method of propaganda for the cause of federal union and the initiation of American colonization, as much as for official orthodoxy. It was in every land the ruling idea of the age to cover politics with the cloak of religion — a game of practical politicians not yet wholly out of use. In Motley's version — which is more of a drama than a history — his comments on this National Synod of Dort approach caricature.

Carolus Nellius, pastor of the Walloon church of Utrecht, made protest, saying that he could not see why the Walloons and Remonstrants had not as

.99

much right to dissent from this Dordrecht Synod, as their forefathers had to dissent from the Council of Trent. When Bogerman, the president of the Synod, lost his temper and with angry gestures drove away the condemned Arminians, Nellius said, "From this injustice of the Synod I appeal to the throne of Christ." Even Prince Maurice, the radical Unionist and relentless foe of Barneveldt and of secession, who was the chief patron of the colonization of America and protector of the Walloon emigrants, was displeased at the violence of Bogerman.

The execution of Barneveldt, which quickly followed, revealed the political animus lurking under religious pretexts. Much Prince Maurice cared for purity of doctrine, or for soundness in morals or religion! Even to-day, while Barneveldt has his memorial reared by the nation — the Queen leading in subscription — Maurice still awaits such an honor by a people who admired his abilities, while outraged by his private life.

In fact, throughout the whole history of the Reformed Church in the Netherlands, the influence of the Walloon Christians was irenic and ever in the line of moderation.

CHAPTER XI
IN THE LANDS OF EXILE

THE story of the flight of the Flemings and Walloons from the southern Netherlands, following the invasion by the Duke of Alva, with his Spanish army of men and women, who came like locusts to devour, has often been told. In "Belgium: The Land of Art," I have tried to picture the scene. Alva has left in Belgium a name of eternal detestation. Even during his lifetime, they tumbled his self-reared statue into the mire. After plentiful pounding with hammers, they cast it into the flames.

On his approach in 1567, which meant not only devastation, but falsehood, treachery, and brutality in high office — done in the name of God and the holy centralized Church — depopulation began.

Even critical authors vary as to the census of the great dispersion. Once more the "fleemings," or Flemings, fled. Once again those called foreigners, or "walloons," became aliens in lands afar. The continent, the near Britain and the distant Norse isles, far-off Russia, and the two continents below the equator received the fugitives, who refused to sell their convictions or their consciences.

Among the very first to give welcome and shelter was England. The Dutch church at Austin Friars in London, "the Church in the Crypt" at Canterbury, and the Walloon church at Norwich, are the oldest among the Reformed churches in England. Yet a score or more congregations of Walloons, whether so-called or termed "French," were gathered in the south and east of England long before the arrival of the Huguenots of France, in 1685 and later. At Southampton, Colchester, and in Threadneedle Street in London were flourishing Walloon churches, and in England more than one Synod was held. The records of some churches extend back to 1568, the first year after the great flight. The Acts of Parliament relating to the Denization and Naturalization for these aliens in England, from 1509 to 1603, form an interesting chapter in the history of civilization.

Yet the number of Walloons who found shelter in the British Isles was but a fraction, compared with that of those who sought temporary or permanent homes in the northern or Dutch Netherlands. Under the Republic's flag of freedom, beneath the folds of which they found protection, thousands of them enlisted to serve and fight for their new Fatherland. It was under this flag, more numerously and oftener than any other, that the Huguenot Walloons fought — thousands of them making "the supreme sacrifice," in the hope of winning for the world and for themselves a larger freedom and a higher obedience.

He misreads history who imagines that the Reformation movement meant a struggle for liberty only. One Netherlands professor has even written a

monograph entitled "Calvinism or Libertinism?"
Some writers still in the mediæval obedience imagine
that the Reformed Churchmen sought only to "raise
discords in Church and State," and to cast off all
restraints and service, in order to enjoy license.

The reality is at the antipodes of such a notion.
The men who made the Bible their sole guide and
authority sought freedom, not as the indolent slave
escapes from labor, but as men taught of God's
Word, as they believed it, in order to submit joy-
fully to a Higher Master and to take on gladly the
yoke of greater service. They left a lower loyalty
for a higher, as all real men do when enlightened.
In proof of this was the universally acknowledged
higher ethical tenor of life among the Huguenots
and the superiority of their economics and material
fruitfulness. This was as manifest as mathematics.
It was demonstrable in visible production, when
those who prayed to saints and counted beads gave
but two hundred days in the year to work, while the
Huguenots devoted three hundred days to toil with
brain and hands.

Thousands of Walloons served in the armies, first
of William the Silent and then of the Republic, when
formed in 1571. The terrible Sea Beggars were
largely from Belgic Land. Treslong, captor of Brill,
the Lexington of the Dutch war of independence,
and Boisot, the rescuer of Leyden, were both of
them Walloons. At the siege of Rouen, by Henry
IV, eight regiments were Walloon; while in 1688, un-

der William III, in England and Ireland, Huguenots made up half his army. After helping to defeat the traitor king James II, many of the veterans of William III remained in Ireland, introducing the crafts of lace- and linen-making and in many ways improving Ulster and North Ireland. Thousands of the "Scotch Irish" of to-day are descended from Belgic and French Huguenots, and bear their names, more or less altered to suit foreign ears and tongues. The registers of the French Conformed Churches of St. Patrick and St. Mary in Dublin — two among those Walloon churches that became Episcopal — were published in 1893.

Until the northern Netherlanders had a national flag, they used the three colors of the prince, orange, white, and blue; which, after 1581, became the national emblem, but later by law was made the red, white, and blue. There were, of course, the arms and heraldry of cities blazoned on the flags which waved in the breezes; for the evolution of the Dutch Republic was in the line of unifying many city republics into a nation. It is true that, when compared with the federal system of the United States of the twentieth century, theirs was a weak federalism; but, such as it was, it served to unite the seven northern provinces. Nearly all our American mottoes and war cries, such as, "No taxation without representation," "E pluribus unum," "The Union must and shall be preserved," "Union makes strength," etc., were heard first in the Netherlands.

IN THE LANDS OF EXILE

The name of "The Church under the Cross," thus chosen, found expression even when the persecuted Belgians called themselves "Beggars," and, driven off the land, took to the sea. The first flag raised by them was white, with a red cross, to signify their homelessness, desolation, and sufferings; meanwhile making the sea very unsafe for Spanish vessels.

When Count Louis, brother of the great William, took up arms against Spain, six of these flags were presented to him. They bore mottoes in Latin, meaning "Now or never," "Regain or die." After 1570, the Beggars of the Sea, many of whom were Walloons, flew the colors of William and also the city flags of the captains. Yet the Netherlanders had their grim jokes. Most comical, as well as defiant, were the broad red pennants flying from every ship. On these were painted ten pennies. This was in derision of Alva's tax of the tenth penny, laid on all business transactions, from which the Beggars were determined to deliver their countrymen.

When Leyden, then full of Walloons, was in course of being relieved, the people not only raised flags on the walls, but fastened these bits of bunting to the highest points of the windmills, in defiance of the Spaniards and in faith of ultimate victory. This cheered the Walloon leader, Admiral Louis de Boisot, of the oncoming cannon boats, manned by Zeelanders and Walloons who were the rescuers. These desperate fellows, every one of whom wore the silver crescent, inscribed "Better Turk than Pope" (or

Papist), read the signal, "Leyden still holds out."
They pushed their boats on through the flood that had
poured through the broken dikes, and they finally
won. The place where they stepped out of their
boats, to throw up loaves and herring to the starving
Leydeners, on October 3, 1574, is still marked; and
near the sluice and bridge stands the House of Archives, in which are so many documents relating to
the Pilgrim Fathers, founders of Massachusetts, and
to the Walloons, founders of New York and the
Middle States. These, in the total, outnumber all
others elsewhere which are dated before 1620.

In the Dutch Republic was the original home of
the "flag," as Americans understand the word and
its association of ideas. Not only the name itself,
but almost the entire vocabulary in English, is derived from the Dutch. The abundant words in other
languages are as reflectors casting light upon this assertion. In their structure, use, and true meaning
they show that the ideas underlying these symbols of
feudal and royal rule, instead of nationality, were
different from those that lay at the foundation of the
national naval flag of the Dutch Republic, which
consisted of seven parallel red and white stripes. Almost for the first time in history, this emblem of sovereignty stood, not for kings, emperors, individuals,
or local rulers, or even for provincial or municipal
entities or persons, but for states.

In a word, the idea of the Dutch flag was federal,
not feudal. It meant equality and unity of the prov-

inces, that were federated out of seven states particular into the one States-General, or the republic formed in 1579 and declared independent in 1581. "Staff," "bunt," "bunting," "fly," "halyards," "stripe," "field" (not canton) are all Dutch. "Stripe," signifying a band of color, was not in the English language before the word having this signification was borrowed from the Dutch. That is the reason why, in the English Bible, Joseph's coat of many "stripes," and the Princess Tamar's "striped" skirt, of which the Hebrew tells us, are rendered by the term "colors" — which does not fill out the idea of Israel's narrators. The wimples, pennants, drapeaux, pavilions, ensigns, banners, colors, etc., etc., of feudal or royal captains, or men-at-arms, were not true flags, in the modern sense of the word, certainly not in that of the Dutch naval flag, or of the American Stars and Stripes — ideas and symbols which to-day have been copied by scores of states and nations.

We may well ask how these people, the ancestors of so many of us, felt when torn from their homes and ancestral surroundings and they found themselves aliens in foreign lands.

Does a prisoner think of freedom, or an exile of home? Long before the Pilgrim Fathers arrived, Leyden was a shelter for many homesick souls from Hainault, Namur, and the southern Belgic provinces. Stripped and impoverished, those of both the first and later generation, fugitives from the Spanish terror, were thankful for the welcome accorded them and the free opportunities offered for "life, liberty, and the pursuit of happiness." Yet they hoped on and hoped ever to return to their old cities and villages. Like the Pilgrim Fathers and Mothers, they suffered the same pangs of homesickness. With them were the same heartaches, in yearning, for years, to see once again the land they loved. The woes of the English exiles, as told by Bradford, have become a world-story. Written as a prose epic, in a classic book and oft recounted, they are known to all; but the sorrows and privations of the first founders of our Middle States were none the less real, while vastly greater in both numbers and length of time.

A second swarming from the old hive — rather the pushing out of the nest by new masters — took place under Louis XIV, even of the Walloons, from soil that was then French, but of old Belgic, after the revocation of the Edict of Nantes. These fled again, with the French Huguenots, into England, Germany, Denmark, Russia, the West Indies, South Africa, and South America, and the Old House of Hospitality, the Dutch Republic. Yet one and all cherished during their lifetime the dream of again regaining the home of their fathers. They ever trusted that the Great Powers would intervene in their behalf and restore to them their farms and cities.

When in 1697 the diplomatists gathered around the green baize table at Ryswick — now a railway station in South Holland, between Delft and The

Hague — to settle terms of peace after war, the Huguenots sent piteous petitions, but they were ignored. To-day on the spot where stood the House of Disappointment, no trace is visible of either the business which made truce, rather than peace, or of the sorrow of those who died in despair.

Again at Utrecht, in 1713, the petitioners for home, freedom, justice, and the rights of conscience appeared, only to be ignored or shown the door. The British masters of statecraft were then more eager apparently to win gold and prestige from the African slave trade, and to outwit Spaniards in man-stealing, than to help poor white refugees. What seem to us the almost idiotic wars of "the Spanish Succession," were made to cease; but British covetousness was confirmed in its "rights"(?). The traders, who were then dominant in Parliament, were guaranteed the virtual monopoly of the capture and sale of human beings. Queen Anne, however, by her personal intervention, secured the release from the French galleys of several score slaves who had held to their faith. One of these wrote the "Confessions of a Protestant."

Happily in later time, the British national conscience was aroused against this iniquity. Then the ethically belated Americans became the target of protest and contempt by the English, because of the "peculiar institution" of slavery continued on Southern soil, when cotton culture demanded an ever enlarging area.

CHAPTER XII
THE WALLOONS ENRICH SWEDEN

Not least among the countries that have sent their sons and daughters to build up the American Commonwealth is the land of Gustavus Adolphus. The Swedes began a colony on the Delaware in 1655. In their more recent and vastly larger contingent of immigrants, who have helped to settle the great Northwest, their record of illiteracy is the smallest among those who seek America.

Besides their intelligence, the Swedes as a whole quickly become very good Americans. Never great psychologists, or students of mental science, they have excelled in the study of nature, and no nation has surpassed them in the number, proportionately, of masters in the domain of science and mechanics. Even their folk songs praise the beauty of nature. They seldom deal with the varied passions and records of humanity, its glories and its foibles. This trait is discernible even in their names. Whereas the English took theirs from trades and occupations, and the Dutch from places, those of Sweden reflect, in their form, the mountains, streams, trees, and flowers of their native land.

Before the Spanish invasion of 1567, even as early as 1560, Walloons had come into Sweden by invitation of Gustavus Wasa, to help in shipbuilding and other industries. One became the private tutor of the young prince Eric XIV. In fact, it was mainly through these Belgic Walloons that the princes and rulers of Sweden became so deeply interested in the "Reformed-" religion. Charles IX, who died in 1612, the father of the great Gustavus Adolphus, was especially earnest in his inquiries and studies of the Calvinistic side of the Reformation. In time, many of these Walloons wrote their names as Waller — whence hundreds of families in English-speaking countries.

We need not then be surprised that the Walloon, besides being teacher, soldier, shipbuilder, unceasing in his industry, showed himself, when in Sweden, a wonder-worker in metals. In fact he created a new art in the mastery of iron.

Not only did the Walloons "improve the iron industry," but they are looked upon as the founders of the whole system of metallurgy; since, before their coming, the art of refining iron and other metals had scarcely begun. Among their ten thousand descendants in the Sweden of our day is the ennobled family of de Geer. In the royal patent granted to the founder, it is expressly stated that "he had introduced the art of casting iron cannon [when formerly only brass had been used], of making bars of malleable iron, of manufacturing all kinds of arms, of building at great expense many factories for brass and iron work, and that he imported many skilled workmen and taught our inhabitants [Swedes] the

secrets of the iron industry." Even the popular histories tell of this economic re-creation of Sweden by
a Walloon.

The story of how all this came about reads like a
romance. Ten years after Alva's invasion of Belgic
Land, and when under a Spanish king and priestcraft
life to the Christians of the Reformed faith had become hardly worth living, Louis de Geer, of Brabant,
became a refugee. He sold his possessions and sent
the money to Amsterdam. Then, traveling secretly
with his wife, eight children, and a loyal servant, he
was able to reach Maastricht, the last station within
the then Spanish Netherlands. There he rented a
river boat, used to freight peat down the Maas
(Meuse) River to Holland. In the boat, back of the
black bricks of this vegetable fuel, he arranged a
little compartment for his family. It was so completely hidden from the inspectors on the frontier
that he got safely across the border into the Dutch
Republic. Stepping on land, they all, father,
mother, children, and servant, fell on their knees and
in the new Fatherland devoutly thanked God for
their escape and their freedom. In Amsterdam, de
Geer started a bank, organized a business house, and
made a fortune. To his estate and to the headship of
the house, the son Louis (1587–1662) succeeded and
in 1617 negotiated a large loan to finance the wars of
Gustavus Adolphus.

Walloons had previously reached Sweden, and a
relative, named de Besche, called the attention of de

THE WALLOONS ENRICH SWEDEN

Geer to the industrial opportunity in Sweden, where skilled labor and educated engineers were lacking for the iron mines. Seizing the opportunity, Louis went to Sweden in 1627 and there made large investments. The Government gave to de Geer the plant at Finspong, which had thus far yielded little; but under de Geer's management it became more profitable than most gold mines.

Into Sweden de Geer brought hundreds of skilled Walloon miners and metal-workers — an enterprise which the Government gladly encouraged. Several of his children settled permanently in the kingdom and were ennobled as barons, as was also de Besche. Not only were the de Geers of Sweden a family highly respected — hundreds in time bearing the name — but from them arose many scientific men, famous for their attainments. The recently published book on the ancestry of the de Geers shows, in sumptuous form, Sweden's great debt to these men.

In the mining and iron industry of our day, names of manifestly Walloon or French origin are common in the directories. This seems to show that, in Sweden, it was not at first so common a custom among the refugees to change their patronyms, as in other lands of asylum, and only recently a popular book has been published in Sweden which gives more details, as follows:

Walloons came from Belgium during the seventeenth century, to improve the Swedish iron industry. They settled near the great iron works in East Gothaland, Upland, Värmland, and Bergslagen. They are represented mostly by a dark type [as compared with the florid blondes], are for the most part of short stature, thickset growth, and have broad faces. They have intermarried among themselves and partly with Swedes, and owing to this a great many types have arisen. The descendants of these Walloons have now spread themselves over the whole country.

At first, besides having their own ministry, teachers, and physicians, they did not marry with the native Swedes. It was nearly a century before they ceased to be "a peculiar people." In modern Sweden, nearly four hundred names of Walloon origin, some of them quite common in America, have been traced out.

What is true of the Swedish is equally so of the American composite. "The melting pot" reveals a similar ingot. Those who have lived in the six Eastern States, still spoken of as "New England," might in like manner describe the very varied physiognomy of American citizens, in that section of the United States, who are descended from ancestors who began at Plymouth to mingle Walloon and French blood with the English, Welsh, Scotch, and Dutch strains. These were efficient in land east of the Hudson, from 1620 to 1776, in altering the legendary, but very much mixed "Anglo-Saxon"; or rather the inherited Celto-Norse-Frisian-Teutonic type of face and form in the British Isles. Certainly the swarthy, brunette coloring of the Walloon is easily discernible in some parts of the United States.

Such, at least, is the impression of one who has

studied the origins and influences operating in the six Eastern States, and who, in addition to seven years of residence in Boston, in which are all of the rural and urban types, visited leisurely the regions from Eastport to Greenwich, and from the Canadian border to Long Island Sound.

One recent Swedish writer has described the Walloons in Sweden as having in most cases dark complexion and brown eyes. They are open and free in conversation, keen in judgment, and apt to learn. They are very touchy in disposition, and often appear a little bit stiff and formal in manner. They dress well and keep their houses scrupulously clean. They are very high-minded and stand above most people in cultural tact.[1]

In his book "The Cradle of Pennsylvania," Mr. T. W. Balch has awarded to the Swedes the honor of first establishing homes in the Keystone State. Before these, however, were the four Walloon brides and their husbands, married on the colonizing ship New Netherland, in 1624. They first saw the future site of the city of Philadelphia, and their homes were on an island in the Delaware River, probably near Trenton. They later lived on the soil of Delaware — which owes its primal existence as a colony and its sovereignty as a state to the Dutch discovery, claim, settlement, and occupation.

Nevertheless, to the Swedes we must award the honors of inaugurating the commonwealth named

[1] E. Hartman, in *Nordisk Familjebok.*

115

after William Penn. The proofs of their life and work on the soil are still in notable evidence to any one who, like the writer, has lived on ground which they occupied within the southern limits of the Quaker city. On February 6, 1909, in the presence of the municipal dignitaries and the representatives of historical and patriotic societies, American and Swedish, a superb bronze tablet, presented by the Society of Colonial Wars, was unveiled at the City Hall in Philadelphia.

No plan for colonizing America was conceived in nobler thought, or dedicated to a higher proposition than this of Gustavus Adolphus and his chancellor Oxenstierna — both among the great men of all time. In the height of his victories, in northern Germany, over the armies of absolutism in Church and State, this great-minded ruler, at Nuremberg, in 1632, drew up a recommendation of this colony as "the jewel of his kingdom." Oxenstierna, looking even further into the future, declared that the results of the colonization of America by men of the North would be "favorable to all Christendom, to Europe, and to the whole world."

Death on the field of battle arrested the project for a time, for the successor of Charles being Christina his daughter, then but six years old, the enterprise was postponed. Her name, in slightly altered form, is to-day borne, not only by the town on the Delaware, Christiana, but by a half dozen other places in the United States.

THE WALLOONS ENRICH SWEDEN

Fitly the Swedes, who during the nineteenth century so largely helped to people the old Northwestern States, have proposed to celebrate in 1923, with a voyage across the Atlantic in a ship of ancient model, the first sailing of their countrymen to America.

Here we may ask: What was the secret of the relative industrial superiority, greater general prosperity, and continuing economic power of the Walloons and the Huguenots? Uprooted from their homes, and compelled to live in strange lands, with the disadvantages of climate and soil, why were such triumphs in civilization wrought by them in both Europe and America?

Two factors from the first were potent to make fresh contributions to civilization and human progress.

The first was the joyousness of the new form of religion, which in itself was but a renewal of that which, in the morning of Christianity, made the faces even of slaves to shine, filled souls with light and brought new raptures, making life vastly more worth living than ever before. This joy was in itself creative.

It is not merely steam, electricity, and commerce that have made a new industrial world, but a new kind of man, who was ever passing on the torch to higher achievements. None illustrated this truth more than those Walloons who, exiled for conscience' sake, went forth, not weeping, or sitting idly at the fountains of the past, but with creative joy in their eyes, to new visions and to new achievements.

In fact very much the same story of the creative industry of the Walloons in the British Isles, Germany, the northern Netherlands, Sweden, South Africa, and the West Indies, might be told of their fellow believers everywhere. In Denmark, for example, in Copenhagen and at Fredericia, the still existing Reformed churches of these places give honor in their histories to "the Walloon period." In Switzerland, both the voluntary refugees and the exiles forced out of the Belgic Netherlands, under Alva and Parma, finding creed, church order, and language already like their own, promptly united themselves with the Reformed congregations. Thus the Swiss churches were notably reinforced. In the great mural monument of the Reformation, several rods long, recently erected in Geneva, on part of what was the old city wall, but newly faced with stone suitable for sculpture in bas-relief, one may read the pictorial history of the Reformation, particularly as shaped by John Calvin. Here the Swiss, the English, the American, the Dutch, German, and other ethnic phases of the recovery of the history of New Testament Christianity have been worthily told by the chisel of the sculptor and the pen of the historian.

CHAPTER XIII

THE FLOATING PURGATORY

THE life of all animate beings, including man, is one of hope and fear.

For centuries in the litanies of Christendom arose this petition: "From the fury of the Norsemen, Good Lord, deliver us." Such a prayer was for deliverance from pagan savages, worshipers of idols, believers in gods that were but magnified men, with the exaggerated passions of the lair and the jungle.

From the era of "the wars of religion" so-called, the prayers of those who lived in fear of the Spanish Inquisition and the French galleys were put up in terror of Christians so-called. To them "the King's religion" meant a suppression of all that made life desirable.

In America, it was the dread of being "chained to the oar" in the galleys of slavery and in a floating hell, ordained by His Most Christian Majesty, Louis XIV, that made Jacob Leisler, the sleepless enemy of this royal slave driver, so popular in New York. It was the strong probability of consignment to a living death in the galleys that struck terror to the Walloons and Huguenots on Manhattan, Staten and Long Islands, and in Schenectady, New Paltz, New Rochelle, and other settlements, and made them, in overwhelming majority, welcome Leisler as a champion.

The galley was a type of ship efficient and valued, especially in the Mediterranean, from very ancient days. It was in use also in the English Channel and "the narrow seas," down to the middle of the eighteenth century. Then, along with the "fire ship," it vanished from naval warfare. From one to two hundred feet long and from thirty to sixty feet wide, propelled by oars, it could be used as a ram, as a floating battery, or to run aside and board an enemy's ship. A galley was of slight use out on the ocean, but for coast defense and the "narrow" seas, it was formidable, either for menace and the alarm of coasts, or for the crash of action. When cannon were invented and mounted on the forward deck, the power and efficiency of the galley were not to be despised.

Inside and below, chained by the leg to the hard seats, the rowers sat, six in a line, working the oars. These were fifty feet long, poised on a pivot, thirty-seven feet of their length being outside and thirteen feet within the ship. The slaves, kept in rhythmic toil, were directed by the officer's whistle. The knotted lash was always ready for welts and blood, but even without that instrument of torture, men often collapsed and died at their task. After each scourging, the stripes and bloody flesh, opened by the rope's end, were washed with salt and vinegar. This caused excruciating agony, but it tended to speedier

A GALLEY
From an old French Print

healing. The corpses were at once flung into the sea. The average life of a rower was ten years. The documentary history and the literature and narratives of those who suffered in the galleys show that the conditions and horrors under the system were not radically different from those of the Middle Passage in the African slave trade.

The slaves, Christian and Mahometan, in the rowing crews, were of a very miscellaneous description. Many were Turks captured by the Levantine corsairs, sold in the slave markets of Italy and bought by the French.

Beside these foreigners, were those native French criminals condemned in the courts under His Most Christian Majesty, by the Inquisitors, and by the civil and military magistrates, for their crimes. Their punishment in hard labor in the galleys was often worse than death. All the galley slaves bore the marks of their degradation, being clothed in red and branded on their flesh with the letters GAL.

But in the purview of "the King's religion" and the kind of a France and French law that existed before the Revolution of 1789, the term "galerien" was given to all convicts. Until this era had passed, a man who exercised his own conscience in worship was deemed worse than a thief or murderer. So there were condemned to the galleys nobles, gentlemen, scholars, and other Christians of the Reformed Church, innocent of all evil — except what was prescribed by the corporation in Italy and reinforced in France.

It was by the French people themselves, that the hated name, with all that it signified, was changed to "forçat" (convict). In the Land of the Bull Fights, the term "galera" is still used for a criminal condemned to penal servitude.

Through the intercession of Queen Anne of England, the French author of the book "Memoirs of a Protestant," by Jean Marteilles, regained his freedom. His book, translated by Oliver Goldsmith, was published, first in Holland, in 1757, and later in England. By this and other writings, the horrors of the galley slave system were made known to the world in vivid and realistic presentation. Nevertheless, after the French Revolution, the realities of this relic of savagery had been so far forgotten that it was exceedingly difficult to find even one copy of the books describing it, so thoroughly had the work of this sort of protestantism against prelatical autocracy been done. Although the phrase "chained to the oar," became a common expression in rhetoric, few of those who in a later time used it thought of any but of Roman history, and as a matter wholly ancient. Yet to-day, as we read the list of the French galley slaves known to the author of "Memoirs of a Protestant," we recognize them as the same as those borne by American families among us and common in the city directories. Another book, written by Jean F. Bion, issued in London in 1708, recounted "the Torments which the French endure, aboard the galleys."

Within the past decade, a correspondent and fellow researcher in the Dutch archives found a list of slaves in the French galleys, the highest number passing thirty-nine thousand.

In colonial America, these dangers of being sent to the floating purgatory established by "the King's religion," had as real an existence as the war whoop of the Algonquin, the cry of the panther, or the rattle of the venomous snake. We may smile now at such fears, for "they jest at scars, who never felt a wound." Even the monster brutalities of St. Bartholomew's are now explained away in American newspapers and encyclopædias, that depend too much on the lucre derived from both circulation, box-office receipts, gate-money and that potent system of bribes — the newspaper advertisements. Nevertheless, we welcome real history, that destroys unjust prejudice and popular notions that obscure facts, revealing truth that heals divisions and unites in holy energy those who serve the same Lord and Master.

CHAPTER XIV

THE ECONOMIC CREATORS OF EUROPE

THE very fact that large classes of the population in Belgium and France — in the main the most intellectual and industrial — were driven out from the lucrative posts and occupations connected with the name of religion, as well as in ordinary industry, released enormous forces for action elsewhere in the building of the modern economic world.

Such expulsion by bigotry was the best conceivable preparation for an age which was soon to come, when, through his own free and disciplined energies, man was to summon to serve him the latent and irresistible forces of nature. Some of these unsuspected powers, such as those which science reveals in steam and electricity, were to be, for the first time in the history of human invention, greater than man himself.

Hitherto such colossal manifestations had existed only in the realms of imagination, in mythology and fairy lore. Now, harnessed potencies, mightier than Samson, Hercules, or even a Frankenstein, were to become the obedient servants of man. The light of suns at unmeasured distances was to be chained to serve him. The vapors of common water were to drive engines and propel ships and cars beyond the might of horses, even though harnessed by the myriads. Ordinary air was made to reveal unsuspected might for common use. The mysterious current hitherto visible to man chiefly in the lightning and audible in thunder, gave the world a new nervous system and made of earth a whispering gallery. An atom was seen to be a miniature universe.

The unseen powers of the cosmos, hitherto thought to be as untamable as the lion or the serpent, were to lie down together and a little child was to lead them. An infant's touch was to blow up the subterranean obstacles of Hell Gate. Out of the alembic of nature, in the heavens among the stars, and from the soil of our planet, were to be summoned new creations in fiber, food, textiles, tools, motors, things of use and beauty, and lines of achievement, which even the ancient seers and interpreters of dreams never in their wildest imagination bodied forth.

In the new era, the Almighty Ruler was lifting the curtain to say, "Behold, I create all things new." Spreading before his children fields and vistas of worlds of old unknown, he was to smile and beckon man on with the invitation, "Concerning the works of my hands, command ye me."

Even of the once mysterious Ocean of Darkness, the Atlantic, stretching westward, the redeemed could sing, "The sea is His and He made it." So trusting the Ruler of the wind and wave, mariners ventured forth to discover new continents. It is no wonder that the first idea, in southern or papal Europe, of a Protestant was that he was a pirate. The vicar of God in Italy had divided the whole world between Spain and Portugal, and were not all oceans in his dominion?

Banished and exiled from all offices and methods of livelihood under "the King's religion," banned even as to marriage, parenthood, assembly, or worship of God at home, the men of the new mind sought other paths of opportunity in fields afar. The French Huguenots followed in the path of the Belgic Walloons. They looked not in vain to the eternal hills, whence their help was to come. They heard the voice, "Behold, I set before you an open door," and even through exile they entered to find peace and prosperity, in the British Isles, the Dutch Republic, Denmark, Sweden, Switzerland, Russia, and Germany. They even sailed beneath the equator to found in South America and South Africa centers of industry. Whether under the Northern Lights or the Southern Cross, they leavened with their joyous spirit and habits of life the communities in which they dwelt.

One might make a varied and lengthy catalogue of the products with which, in every line of human achievement and industry, they surprised the European nations.

In England, the paper, glass, textiles, dyes, products of the soil, improved plants in the garden, whether exotics or staples, with the newly applied results of experience in trade, finance, state, and warcraft, changed Great Britain from an agricultural to a manufacturing and colonizing nation. What they did for England was felt also in Scotland, Wales, and Ireland, in each of which countries thousands of refugees, whose tongue was French, settled. The southern "Irish Walloon" soldier, the Scotch dyer, the northern Hibernian maker of lace and linen, the Welsh sailor and explorer — who was very often one of continental ancestry — carried the fame of the Huguenot to the ends of the earth. Thousands to-day who bear names first heard and written in Hainault, Liège, or the Ardennes — who are "lost tribes," so far as it concerns their own personal knowledge of recorded genealogy — wonder how it came about that their known ancestors were "British," of the three or four kinds; while yet they bear names that are unmistakably French or Walloon in form. And this, despite those phonetic transformations that outrival in wondrous shapes the things and forms of life that suffer the "sea change" of which Shakespeare makes Ariel sing and tell. The numerous statutes of England relating to the denization and naturalization of allies make interesting reading to the student of the progress of civilization.

In Germany, out of the hegira of Walloon and Huguenot scholars, merchants, soldiers,. artisans, agriculturalists, the Great Elector, Frederick William, embodied a French state in his realm. At Berlin and Cologne, and in probably a score of other cities, a multitude of these immigrant craftsmen "introduced arts previously unknown to the ruder civil-

ization of the North." These newcomers made the
rivers of Prussia arteries of trade! They opened the
mines and diverted to Germany the skill and metallic products, for which the western countries had
been so long noted. Prussia's regiments were mightily reinforced by these refugees, and her military
power made more efficient by exiled officers. In the
noble families, courtesy became prevailingly the
rule, because the new immigration was "solid and
civilizing." Nor were any schools in the Empire
equal to those founded by the foreigners, whose polished language became that of the court and diplomacy. The Elector promoted the study and publication of French literature. Nor does Reginald Poole,
who wrote on "The Huguenots in Dispersion," err
in asserting that "the society of Berlin was . . . the
creation of the exile, and it was the refugees that
gave it that mobile course of thought, that finer culture, that taste in matters of art, that instinct of
conversation, which had been the unique possession
of the French. They diffused their own spirit —
quick, fine, lucid, the spirit of French vivacity and
precision."

What one may tell of Prussia, he may truly affirm
of Russia, as any one who has studied the "address
books," or city directories, of Petrograd and other
Muscovite cities — which were most appropriately
published in French — knows well. From the days
of Peter the Great to the Treaty of Portsmouth in
1905, when the Baron de Rosen, great grandson of a

Huguenot, sat opposite Count Komura — one of the writer's pupils during three years in Tokyo — French and Huguenot influences have leavened Russia for the better.

Of Sweden, the story of the Walloon who created the modern iron industry, in both mining and metal working, is told elsewhere. The narrative of how Denmark was leavened for the better and French-speaking churches formed and still maintained in Copenhagen is of absorbing interest. Into the hospitable Republic, the stream of immigration was continuous and ever-increasing, until America helped to absorb the mass of people from France and Belgic Land. Apart from the infusion into the Dutch East India colonies and the revenue accruing from the Greenland fisheries, the flourishing book trade in French and the outpoured literature in that tongue tell their own story. One need not wonder at the exceedingly numerous names, of French and Belgic origin, to be read to-day in the city and town directories of Queen Wilhelmina's realm, or in what was once New Netherland, or in the Eastern, Middle, and Southern States of the American Commonwealth.

As seen in our day, in the perspective of three centuries, the historical situation was wonderfully like that in the year 487 B.C. Then, in prophetic vision, two eras of civilization began, of which the world now beholds the issues and results. It was the setting, in humanity's stadium, of two athletes, that were to race down the centuries and fling their torches into the ages to come. Even after the land and temples of both have been long under the heels of the conquerors, their stories told and their careers ended, we see what the seer meant when, twenty-seven hundred years ago, he gave the word, and they were off in the race: "Thy sons, O Zion, against thy sons, O Greece." Yet to-day, after the fleeting centuries, which civilization gave our race the greater blessing, while flinging forward the torch of democracy's progress for the remaking of the world unto ever-increasing spiritual solidarity?

Neither Walloons nor Huguenots were disobedient to the heavenly vision, nor deaf to the Voice that called. Both went forth, scarce knowing whither they went, yet with songs in their mouths and unending gladness upon their heads, to face duty with the creative eye and hand and to bring blessings wherever they set foot. Let us never forget that the Belgic Walloon was the pilot, predecessor, and exemplar of success to the French Huguenot, even as the Pilgrim set the mark and beacon for the Puritan.

Yet, while nine nations and three continents gratefully confess their deep debt to Walloon and Huguenot, in the crown of their achievements, may there not also be set on their heads the supreme jewel of the colonization of North America? It is to the Huguenots that we owe the idea of fashioning the wilderness beyond the Atlantic into a garden, and creating on the new continent a Protestant nation, a commonwealth of mental freedom, a land

130

ECONOMIC CREATORS OF EUROPE

of schools unshackled by priest or bigot, while constructing a temple of ordered civil liberty.

The dream of the United States of America, free from feudal rulers, kings, emperors, or political prelates, may not have taken shape in the mind of Admiral Coligny; but it is to the French, and not to the English, that we owe the initial peopling of the Northern half of the American continent by men instinct with love of freedom. Nor has any one made more generous acknowledgment of both fact and truth in this matter than Sidney Lee, who led all his countrymen in drawing the map and telling the story of British achievement in the great "Dictionary of National Biography." In addition to his colossal tasks, he wrote thus in "Scribner's Magazine," for June, 1907:

The vision of religious liberty in the new world is a Huguenot creation. It was slow to acquire stern enough sway over the minds of Englishmen to move them to action. . . . The word written and spoken in France of the Calvinistic colonies did penetrating work in England. The beginnings of New England were cast in the Huguenot mould. The great American project of Puritan England differed from the French schemes in Brazil and Florida, neither in motive nor in principle, but [only] in practical achievement and enduring triumph. From the colonial failures of Protestant France followed the colonial success of Protestant England.

It was in the Huguenot spirit that the Puritans of England, when penal legislation drove them from their homes [after hospitable welcome in the Dutch Republic] looked to America for protection and salvation.

THE STORY OF THE WALLOONS

It was Gaspard de Coligny, the great Admiral of France, who shared the vision of the Hebrew prophet of 487 B.C., when the latter set in dramatic contrast the equipment of the two athletes, Greece and Judah, as they started on their career down the ages — the one representing arms and physical force in the phalanx, the other the spirit of peace and altruism in the law and the prophets.

On the die cut for the memorial stamps and the coin struck from the national mint, to celebrate in America the Walloon Tercentenary, there should be the image of the French Admiral Coligny.

Not the least notable of the achievements of Reformed Churchmen was in theology and literature. Yet none of their most important books escaped the attention of the centralized autocracy in Italy, by which a new form of repression was organized.

Only the slow lapse of the centuries was to reveal the results of this law and ban which in the name of God was laid upon the human mind and spirit. Alarmed at the intellect, scholarship, power of mental discipline, and literary attractiveness of the books published by the Free Churchmen, led by Calvin, the father of the modern public school, the papal dynasty proceeded further to fetter the human intellect. Hence the founding and proclamation of the Index Expurgatorius of prohibited books. To read one of the publications of the Free Churchmen, thus banned, through a majority vote in secret conclave,

132

by a bureau in the Italian city, was alleged to imperil the soul's salvation. A priest must first secure permission of his bishop, before he could, without danger of eternal damnation, peruse the publication of the Reformers.

CHAPTER XV

JESSE DE FOREST AND THE SHIP
NEW NETHERLAND

JESSE DE FOREST,[1] a fugitive Walloon, the potential founder of New York, had for years looked for a home in the New World, but he did not at first apply for aid and transportation to the States-General, for until 1621 there was no West India Company. Usselinx, a Belgian refugee in the Republic, had persistently agitated with pen and voice the scheme of such an armed trading and colonizing corporation, for the colonization of America as a checkmate to Spain. Yet this was the very idea against which the great Barneveldt was fighting.

The East India Company, formed in 1595, had no jurisdiction over America, nor any intent to colonize it. In 1609, their great purpose was to find a shorter route to Japan, China, and the East Indies. To this end, encouraged by the Walloon, Peter Plancius, they commissioned the intrepid English pilot, Henry Hudson, in the Half Moon. This ship, named after the silver omen of victory of the invincible, self-named Beggars, entered the waters of what was to be [Terra] Nova Belgica. To this day the Dutch speak of the crescent as "halve maen."

[1] His story, as far as known, is told in *A Walloon Family in America*, by Mrs. Robert W. de Forest, 2 vols., New York, 1914.

JESSE DE FOREST

Hudson sailed first towards the North Pole, but finding himself shut in by icebergs ahead and confronted with mutiny, turned his prow westward, hoping, beyond America, to find China. With this end in view, he sailed into the waters of the Middle States.

By 1619, the Union cause in the Federal Republic of the United Netherlands — the real question at issue being hidden from most historians by the smoke screen of theology — had triumphed. The perils of state right and secession were over, and the men of the new mind were ready to turn faith into sight and hope into fruition.

Those politicians whose entire intellect was concentrated upon protocols, documents, and legal routine, and hence could not discern that the Dutch people had become a commonwealth, a nation, and not merely a huddle of sovereignties, or an agglomeration of political units, had lost in the clash. Both sides, in their faults and their political convictions, and in the violence of their passions, were in a state of degradation beastward, even to bloodthirstiness. In this general wrongheadedness, they were equally men of their times. The sects, in their undisciplined energies, and "the churchmen," so-called, were rivals in the same reversion and path that lead not to Heaven. Barneveldt was beheaded.

In the Netherlands, there were statesmen who realized that however faulty and imperfect the federal union of 1579 might be, nationality and enterprise, with something more than the assertion of state right and stimulus of the home market in Europe, were needed for higher purposes. There must be not only resistance to Spanish despotism, but the creation of a true commonwealth, and the safeguarding of its existence.

With release of pent-up energies and with Walloon and Fleming reinforcement, an advance along the whole line was ordered against Spain — the giant now refreshed for a new onslaught against liberty, after the Great Truce, from 1609 to 1621.

The progressive Union men resolved that the unleashed powers of both war in armed ships and peace in colonization should be carried across the seas, even into America; which Spain, by papal decree, claimed as her sole property. The new continent from pole to pole lay under the Spanish scepter and ban. All except Spaniards were deemed common poachers, burglars, or thieves, if found anywhere in America.

To wrest this scepter from the Land of the Inquisition, of gloomy fanaticism, of bull-fighters and slave catchers, to cast that scepter into the sea, and to free America from Spanish ideals, the men under the orange, white, and blue flag of the Dutch Republic went forth to do a work which was completed under President McKinley, in 1898.

Yet this invasion was to be less by warships loaded with artillery and soldiers, than by peaceful families, even those who in the long run were to conquer wild nature and savage man by tilling the soil,

making homes, and rearing family altars, school-
houses, and churches. It is a pity that Motley
and most writers treat the conflict in the Netherlands, between the forces represented by Maurice
and Barneveldt, as almost wholly theological, and
the long struggle on our continent between Latin
and Germanic types of civilization, for the possession of North America, as chiefly military and stra-
tegic.

In the former case at Dordrecht, in 1619, the conflict was political, envenomed by theology; in the
latter, it was mainly social and economic. On American soil, it was between feudalism and family life,
even more than of forms of either politics or religion.
It was a fair test of ultimate success between free
churchmen and adherents to the papacy.

In 1619, at the end of the Twelve Years' Truce
and in view of the imminent onslaught of the reinforced Spaniards, the Dutch government, needing
every ship, cartridge, and cannon, could not spare
the two men-of-war asked for by the English Separatists, to convoy the Speedwell and Mayflower to the
Hudson River region, in which they expected to
locate. In 1623, however, the States-General was
ready to detach an armed yacht to convoy one of the
West India Company's colonizing ships to the same
region, should colonists be enrolled to go thither.
The fur trade was a monopoly, and the settlers,
whose passage was thus furnished free, must go
out, not as "the summer soldier and the sunshine

patriot," who returned home in winter. They must agree to be farmers or servants and remain on the soil. So, not as the commercial or fishing adventurers, but as home-makers, as permanent settlers, they sailed over the sea, as the pioneers of Christian civilization.

Few natives who had Dutch grandfathers wished at that time to tempt the risks of ocean and wilderness, when the home soil was so fertile, and when industry, to use their own word, was "booming." Moreover, the Dutch fully believed that the Spaniard, who had been once beaten to his knees, would again be humbled by the triumphant Republic, their freedom be fully won, and life more than ever be worth living on ancestral soil. They had already stood confiscation, killing, and burning for over forty years. Now, with true Dutch pluck, they were ready for another grapple and to stand forty years more, if need be, for a fight to a finish.

Yet to make sure of winning, it must be a case of *eendracht magt macht*, that is, of the one pull all together that makes might. Such being the situation, what good would it yield, if even a courageous leader should apply for Government aid in ships and for the resources that were necessary to make a success? Most colonial enterprises, thus far attempted, had spelled starvation.

Such a leader, who combined vision with daring and an indomitable will, stood forth. He was Jesse de Forest, a Walloon. Did he hate the Spaniard and long to help in humbling despotism, through hallowing American soil, by free worship and by honorable toil? Would he help pure religion, while providing a home for his children and for posterity?

Long before 1620 he had begun to dream. In Leyden, this Walloon was established as an expert dyer. He had welcomed those later comers, the Free Churchmen outcast from England, their own country, because they would not sell their consciences for pelf or ease.[1] After all the doors of the home land had been tightly shut and kept barred, they too had looked to America and for a home in the wilderness. They would perpetuate on the new continent the best traditions of English freedom, for they held the future. To-day, after so long a time, England is proud enough of the Pilgrims.

The subject of colonization had been discussed by the Leyden Walloons for years. Most probably Jesse de Forest saw the picked adventurers bound for America — only the young and the strong, for the older ones stayed in Leyden — loading the boats in the canal at the end of the Rapenburg, for the inland voyage to join the Speedwell, at Delfshaven. Then he applied to King James of England to per-

---

[1] Bradford's *History of the Plymouth Plantation* shows us how close in the Republic were the relations of the "French" (Walloon) and the Separatist churches, and J. G. de Hoop Scheffer's *History of the Free Churchmen* [Brownists, Congregationalists, and Baptists], edited by W. E. Griffis (Ithaca, New York, 1922), has still more abundant references to the English and Belgic refugees who held a common faith. By the end of the eighteenth century, the Walloon churches in the Republic numbered sixty-eight.

mit fifty or sixty families, three hundred people in all, as well Walloons as French, and all of the Reformed Church, to be allowed to settle in "Virginia." He also prayed His Majesty to furnish protection, transportation, and defense from and against all enemies, and to maintain them in their religion.

That domain, named after the Virgin Queen Elizabeth, meant the geographical space anywhere and everywhere included on the continent claimed by England because of Cabot's voyage of 1497; but among the Dutch, "the West Indies" was then the common name for America. The application of the Leyden Walloons was sent in the form of a round robin to "the wisest fool in Christendom," through the British envoy, Sir Dudley Carleton. This was the same gentleman who had had the tilt with Elder Brewster over the matter of printing, which, in the main, was free in the Republic, but in England was licensed by royalty and the prelates only. These Walloons wished to plant a colony and keep together in one place, using their own language and form of worship. Jesse de Forest, in the document — which can still be seen among the records in London — was a "certaine Walon."

But de Forest's proposition was too liberal, or too specific, for the English of that day, whether represented by King, Court, Church, or Trading Company. The influences of bigotry were hardening into that settled policy which kept back from America

JESSE DE FOREST

John Robinson, the large-minded and big-hearted pastor of the Pilgrim Fathers.

Yet no light affair, such as the refusal of the king or a corporation, could chill the dauntless spirit of such a man as Jesse de Forest. He had given up his home for conscience' sake, and had, over and over again, bided his time, until finally the opportunity came. In 1620, when the idea of nationalism had triumphed over that of sectionalism, or secession, and not one stripe had been struck from the Union flag, the Dutch West India Company was formed. The dream of Usselinx, the Walloon, had become reality. The time was ripe and American colonization was settled upon as the policy of the Republic. If the two hundred or more Englishmen left behind in Leyden, who were uncertain of their sovereign's mind — their only hope being that he would wink at their venture — were bold enough to tempt the stormy ocean, as they kept on doing, from 1621 to 1630, who could keep back a Walloon — ever the typical man of alert mind?

The new, clean ship, New Netherland, was built by the Dutch West India Company to convey this Walloon colony to America. If pure faith and high principles were as favoring winds, then no craft, before A.D. 1623, crossed the Atlantic with nobler propulsion.

The national colors that floated at her mizzen were those of a federal republic. It was the first flag in northern Europe which was independent of persons, whether prelates, feudal rulers, or sovereigns. It represented seven states in federation, a commonwealth. This flew to the breeze. Their mottoes were "Union makes strength," and "By concord, little things become great," while the piety of these argonauts was expressed in fervency, "Nisi Dominus frustra"— the title words of Psalm cxxvii — which were sung in their devotions and shown in their world. Expanded from the initial words, this meant, "Except the Lord build the city, they labor in vain that build it." These Walloon voyagers were not mere dreamers. Their idealism was laid upon an unshakable basis. "They looked for a city, which hath foundations."

At the peak of the foremast was the proud flag of the armed corporation, "ready for a fight or a frolic," or a victory through industry. It bore the monogram G. W. C., meaning the Chartered (Geoctrooyd) West India Company, not of "Holland," but of the Republic of the United Netherlands.

Of this monster trading corporation — besides possessing powers on land and sea, especially those of war, for defense against Dunkirk pirates, Spanish galleons, and hostile savages, whether called Christian or pagan — it was expected and ordered that first of all, recognition should be made of our common humanity; that is, the fair treatment of the aborigines as men, whatever their condition, creed, or color.

Every square acre occupied by the settlers must

be paid for. It was a case, not of "may," but of "must," in this duty of extinguishing aboriginal claims to the soil; while the instruction of the natives, as far as possible, in Christianity, was also made obligatory. In addition, the Company must provide both the minister and the school teacher. On board the ship New Netherland was the Church officer, consoler of the sick, leader of song, and conductor of worship, with license to marry couples; for among these colonists home-making was the supreme idea as the basis of society.

It is true that these Walloons, so far as detailed and complete records are concerned, stand in history clothed, as it were, with but fig leaves as compared with the full robes of the Pilgrim Fathers, who wear the vestments of Bradford. Comparatively few are the relics and verbal fossils, even as recognized in the names of their descendants and the places upon which they settled. The reason is plain. They had none among them like Bradford, to tell, even to minute particulars, their own story and clothe their venture of faith with the literary garb of subjective opinion, and even of self-flattery, sentiment, and romance. Nor is their own literature of polemics or defense against enemies voluminous. They had none behind, in the country they had left, to vilify and caricature them. Despite the hatred of ecclesiastics who used their own speech to pursue them, the tradition of them in their former home faded as did that of the Pilgrims at Scrooby. Like good beginners of a better time, they gave up, ultimately, their own language and united with their neighbors to build the states in which they had found refuge.

We have no sure proof that any of the colonizers of 1624 settled on Manhattan, though later, some who came in the ships New Netherland or Unity made their homes there along with many others. Until the name of the future city (not the fort) was adopted as New Amsterdam, the island settlement was affectionately spoken of as New Avesnes, after the birthplace of their leader, Jesse de Forest.

No company of American colonizers was more devout, none more pure in morals, nor was there one more ready to acknowledge the mercies of God, or the possibilities of good in man. The intimate life of the churches in New Netherland and their records fear no comparison with those of colonial New England, or the southland. Certainly no hands were readier, no feet more jubilant in helping to build the American Commonwealth, than those of these grateful children of faith and daring. One has but to scan the documents of church and town and the muster rolls of colonial and later wars, or of the Revolution, or those down to 1918, or the lists of patrons, benefactors, or educators, and of able men and women, and count up the shining names on the Nation's bead roll to be convinced of this. The record of the Walloons and Huguenots, in American history, is excelled by none. Yet though their light has been too long hidden, under bushels variously named, we can discern in the spectrum of critical research the superb bright lines of their story.

We do not read of these argonauts of 1624 having arms, swords, or muskets, or of any desire to use them on the natives. They trusted more to their determination to do justice with the red men, and the sequel of success shows that they trusted not in vain.

It would reward the critical student to search and make comparison of the results of the fire-and-sword policy in dealing with the Indians, with those following the methods of the Prince of Peace. Surely Lincoln spoke not in vain concerning the negro slave, and our Government records show that while it has cost us a million dollars to kill an Indian, a mere fraction of this sum now educates him. Would that the spirit and praise of Roger Williams, Peter Minuit, and William Penn had always been followed!

However varied, in blood and creed, in economic condition, or mental equipment, may have been the colonists of North America — numbering in their nationalities at least a score — or however we may lack the exact details of their previous life at home or on shipboard, or of their creeds, or their motives in leaving their old home for the New World, of this common truth we may be sure: one and all, in each case, they followed at first the customs and traditions of their native lands. They had the same infirmities, ideas, notions, convictions, and specters of the brain which were dominant in their ancestors and in the old lands. Hence their actions tallied with their mental acquirements, heritages, and outlook.

Nevertheless, after subjecting to the hottest fires of criticism the "makers of America" — that is, the United States — before 1790, and exposing their limitations, with all their faults and infirmities, one can be sure that, in overwhelming majority, they were from the countries or the peoples that accepted the principles of the Reformation. These principles, when fully worked out, meant the separation of Church and State, a free press, free public schools sustained by taxation, no interference with the consciences of men so long as they were law-abiding; self-government in the commonwealth, and absolute freedom from any European potentate in either Church or State, with unquestioning loyalty to the constitution and laws as made by "the people of the United States."

Once inside Sandy Hook, and past the Island of the States, the ship New Netherland from Amsterdam, after leaving small colonies on two of the islands, Long and Staten, ploughed her way northward. Through the rippling "River Flowing out of the Mountains," then flush with the water of the melted snows of spring-time, they sailed on. The eyes of the colonists had never fallen on such a majestic stream, so imposing also in its environment. In its navigable length it far excelled the Scheldt, the Meuse, or the Sambre.

Nor had these Walloon pioneers ever made so long an inland or river voyage. Past the Palisades, through the Highlands, in the shadows of the Cat- skills they moved, and then the ship beat its way through the low meadowland. At last they came to look upon the site that might be as truly called Tre- mont, as was Boston; for the contour of the land in their new home showed the three distinct slopes, with ravines between the ridges — now hidden by houses, and over which are viaducts, from hilltop to hilltop.

At the base of the hills, they erected their bark cabins. Neither here nor at Plymouth — in spite of the blunders of inaccurate artists, too fond of mere quaintness and oddities — was the log cabin the in- itial type of domestic architecture. After the primi- tive bark dwelling, the later huts were of roughly dressed planks, and the still later edifices were of brick and stone. Those which were visible to the writer in 1866, or which still remain, show in beams and girders the marks of the broad-axe. New Paltz and Kingston have the larger number of these sur- vivals of colonial architecture.

The members of Jesse de Forest's company in the ship New Netherland were the first regular, per- manent colonists in any number who made homes in New Netherland. They were the first to come di- rectly under the law and regulations of the Dutch Republic and to obtain valid land titles. Whether any of them settled on Manhattan is of far less historical importance than is the cardinal fact that they made their homes in New Netherland, on the soil of the four States of New York, New Jersey, Pennsylvania, and Delaware. The four couples married on the ship were put on a yacht, and, ascending Delaware Bay and River, settled on an island near Trenton and later lived on the soil of Delaware, which owes its statehood to the Dutch occupation.

Between the years 1609 and 1623, there had been various spasmodic visits of ships and men, and even of women, to New Netherland. There were even temporary habitations built and fields sown and tilled for food. The Netherlands Trading Company had been chartered for trade and under it a fort or two were built as trading posts. Among these visitors, explorers, traders, or even farmers, before 1623 and 1624, were Walloons, who, however, came from the seven states of the Northern Netherlands and were registered as citizens of the Dutch Republic.

With these sporadic visits, with the activities of individuals, or the Netherlands Trading Company, or even with the first occupation of Manhattan, or of any other island in the archipelago at the mouth of the Hudson River, however important these matters may seem to-day, to the inhabitants of one State or city, our narrative does not concern itself. The basic fact is that during the Twelve Years' Truce between Spain which claimed all America and the triumphant Republic, the Dutch Government authorities could not honorably enter upon the enterprise of American colonization, grant land titles, or in any way legally authorize the formal colonization of a continent claimed by Spain. Nor did they. The States-General took no official oversight of the visitors to or denizens of New Netherland, granted no certificates of private ownership of the soil, nor in any way violated in letter or spirit their plighted good faith, or the terms of the Twelve Years' Truce with Spain. Both governments honorably observed their agreements.

But the National Synod of Dort — held against Barneveldt's state right provincial and peace policy and the wishes of the Arminians and carried to completion by Maurice, backed by the Calvinists and the Unionists — cleared the ground. The West India Company was formed and the colonization — not of Manhattan, nor of the Delaware River island, nor of any specified site or portion, but of New Netherland — was decided upon and the colonizing ship, named after the new province, was built. To execute the national decision of the States-General, it was decreed that a civil government and land titles should be given to the settlers and the new *terra*, or land, be named Nova Belgica. The classic, oldest, most honored name of the country, antedating conquerors, feudal rulers, thrones, kings, or even republics, and in recognition of the people and the soil, was chosen for the seal of New Belgium (Sigillum Novi Belgii). It was not an accident that the first governor was chosen from among the people whom

THE STORY OF THE WALLOONS

William the Silent had hoped to incorporate in the Republic of seventeen states, the Walloon, Peter Minuit. So it came to pass that the colony on the area of what afterwards became the four States of Pennsylvania, New Jersey, Delaware, and New York, formed the only group of settlements that was under one government, and that of a republic.

CHAPTER XVI

MAKING THE WILDERNESS BLOOM

WITH those industrious habits that are second nature to a Walloon, the men of the eighteen families settled at Fort Orange, the future site of Albany, and began at once to tickle the earth to make it laugh with harvests. With houses to build, the ground to plough and harrow, and homes to equip with comforts, the days sped swiftly by and sleep at night was sound. Sky and river, fruitful earth, and pleasant climate made the new life a joy. They missed the chimes at hours and quarters, the carillons making music in the air, the old surroundings of art and culture, and the grand edifices, civic and ecclesiastical, of the home land; but they were happy with new visions of peace, freedom, and prosperity. With the true spirit of pioneers, these people, of piety, faith, and industry, led the van of Distinctive America. They had in them, deeply rooted, that which best makes the foundations of a state secure — family life, industry, and religion. Moreover, they were not discontented ladies and gentlemen seeking gold and luxury, but plain people willing to toil. They considered life worth living only when the primeval law of eating one's bread in the sweat of the face was obeyed.

There is no drapery of mythology, sentimental

conceit, or swollen family pride about what was brought over in the ship New Netherland, nor even vulgar notions and popular superstitions, which grow, like fungus on a dead log, and, long after the event, real or imaginary, furnish food for the novel, the pageant, the drama, or the moving picture shows. Little furniture and not many extant relics came over in the vessel. Yet the scene and the emotions of those who, with their families, first saw the sites of the future cities of New York, Brooklyn, Albany, and Philadelphia are not without trustworthy tradition.

The Walloons won friends at once. They did not lie awake at midnight in terror, listening to the blood-curdling war-whoop of the oncoming savage. Even before they reached their bourne, the first link in the silver chain of friendship between the red and the white man, which in Iroquois oratory and practice was to be "brightened" again and again, had been forged. As early as 1614, the Dutch commander, after satisfying the natives' claim of ownership of the land, had made a covenant of peace with the lords of the Long House.

It may be that there was no altruism, or indeed any noble sentiment, on either side, in this compact of friendship with the Five Nations. The Iroquois sought the friendship of the Dutch for the sake of firearms and for vengeance against the Hurons, their old enemies, and their new ones, the Canadian French, and the Dutch wanted furs. Long are the memories of injured men! The Iroquois had never forgotten the deadly interference of Champlain and his comrades dressed in iron clothes, and with iron tubes charged with lightning and thunder, when on the lake shore the northern and southern men of the Stone Age had met in battle. The clash of conflict at long range, against the warriors of the Long House, was decisive; but not because of superior war craft, or the valor of the Hurons. It had come about because of the white men's partisanship and their new weapons, which killed invisibly at a distance, when no bowstring had twanged or spear had been hurled.

The Iroquois, having from the first been treated like fellow human beings, were determined to safeguard the friendship of the men who could not only trade with them, but also vitally help them. Hence the "Covenant of Corlaer" lasted much longer even than Penn's covenant with the Lenni Lenape Indians — so praised by Voltaire — even until the nineteenth century. Then in 1874, the League of the Iroquois itself, in the presence of ex-President Fillmore and some of the highly civilized descendants of the Indians — ladies and gentlemen of rank and fashion — was dissolved. The friendship of red and white men in New York perdured. This "Covenant of Corlaer" became a barrier to French-Canadian aggression and was one of the factors deciding Anglo-Saxon domination in North America.

It happened that shortly after the arrival of the

THE STORY OF THE WALLOONS

Walloons, at Beverwyck, a war party of the Mohicans, following the bad example of the Hurons with Champlain, tested friendship on a new venture, by making use of their Dutch neighbors as allies. They requested Commander Daniel K. Krieckenbeeck, with six of his garrison, to go with them on the warpath. Of the white men, one was known to be from Hoorn, in North Holland, and two were Portuguese. The two bodies of armed men marched together.

The Dutch, having guns, were probably in the van. When about three miles out, they either met with an ambuscade, or in the open faced a sudden and furious onslaught from the Mohawks, who attacked with a shower of arrows. The commander of the fort, three of his men and many of the Mohicans were killed.

The Iroquois at this time, like our own far-off pagan ancestors, were occasional cannibals, but the cannibalism of the American Indians — as Mary Jamison, the illustrious captive, has explained to us — had a religious significance; as probably was the case among all ancient man-eating or man-burning nations. Cremation was made to propitiate the spirits of their own slain warriors and to satisfy their families and kinsfolk, who mourned for the lost, while the feasting was to gain the courage of brave foes. In addition, the Mohawks carried back home a leg and an arm, to be divided among bereaved relatives in condolence and as a sign that their enemies had been overcome.

154

MAKING THE WILDERNESS BLOOM

In this case, after duly roasting, the cooked victim was Tymen Bouwensz. The other bodies of the slain natives they gave to cremation. The three dead Dutchmen were buried together. One of the two Portuguese, who tried to escape by swimming, was hit by a shaft sped from an Indian archer. Though wounded in the back, the swimmer succeeded in getting away.

Here was a clear case of unwarranted intermeddling on the part of the foreigners; for later the Mohawks solemnly declared that there was with them no malice aforethought against the white men. Only a few days after the fight, the skipper, Peter Barentz, visited them, probably at their village of Schenectady. On coming back, he reported that "they wished to excuse their acts, on the plea that they had never set themselves against the whites, and asked the reason why the latter had meddled with them; otherwise, they would not have shot them."

Because of such dangers, between savage tribes ever at war — though probably these dangers were more imaginary than real — these pioneer Walloon families were, after a while, removed for safety to Manhattan. The Dutch Director, determined on successful colonization, made a "concentration"; but sometime afterwards, when the situation was fully understood, probably most of them returned to their first allotment. When fourscore years had passed, the first-born baby girl, then an old woman, Catalina Trico, testified that she had lived for three years in Beverwyck, as this settlement was called, after its chief staple, beaver fur, and during this time "the Indians were as quiet as lambs."

Modern science does not permit the scholar, who has studied man in his evolution, to consider everything in savage life, or among men without writing, as necessarily or intrinsically lower than the standards of the white man. Nor can it even be proved that the Indian, especially the Iroquois, was less original than the white man's own ancestors when in the Stone Age. It is interesting to note that within a short distance of the Walloons' initial settlement was the classic Tawasentha, the legendary home of Hiawatha, the culture-father of the Iroquois, whom Longfellow has celebrated. Close at hand, also, was the beautiful valley of Norman's Kill, where the children, red and white, played together.

While the wijk, or town, was named after the Beaver (which in Dutch is Bever), the usual local term was the Fuyck (a bow-net), because, in its shape, the new settlement resembled the bow-net or fishtrap, then in common use, which kept fresh food on their tables. It rhymes with wijk.

They were now in the country of the Mohicans, whom Cooper was to glorify, and on the opposite side of the river was one of the red men's palisaded structures. This site and neighborhood is the Greenbush of to-day, and here in later times was the home of "Yankee Doodle." The Mohicans were different in blood and language from the Iroquois, but formed a part of the great Algonquin community. This like an ocean surrounded the island-like League of the Five Nations of the Iroquois, whose habitat was at that date comparatively small in area, though superbly situated for defense or strategy. From their great natural castle, on the ridge and western flats, extending from Niagara to the Hudson, in the citadel of America, with its forty-nine valleys, all admirable sally ports, this agricultural community dominated many tribes in every direction.

The advent of the European interrupted the evolution of the native American, and in the main deflected its course in paths that meant degradation and destruction. With firearms, the Iroquois were already becoming expert gunmen and in time were to terrorize the land, even to the menace of Montreal. They carried their scalping knives beyond the Connecticut River, on the one hand, and to the Mississippi River on the other, but with fiery liquor and new diseases under the persistent pressure of the covetous white man, the red man lost vastly more than he had gained.

Whether or not the newcomers brought cradles — the very name is Celtic, or Walloon — we cannot tell, but they soon had need of them. The little Americans could not be carried on their mothers' backs, like papooses, or hung on trees to swing in the breezes. They must the rather be content with birch bark cradles, or those made from staves or kegs with semicircular rockers, once part of the

157

heads of the kegs or barrels. Yet of all the babies born on the American continent, dandled on mothers' knees, or sung to sleep with lullabies; or pleased little folks amused with rhymes, or the rattles of language, or the lore of Santa Claas and of fairy folk, not one set was more richly provided than the babies in Nova Belgica; for no land is more affluent in legends of St. Nicholas and in the rhymes of the children inviting or praising their patron saint, than is that of the Belgic Netherlands.

Happily, though many historiographers, careless scholars, many books, and even tablets of bronze and stone, talk of the non-existent New Netherlands, when Nova Belgica was only one province of the Republic, these early documents preserve for us in text and speech the name Nieuw Nederlandt, or, in English, New Netherland, and none of them makes the mistake of calling a Domine a "dominie," for the clerks and chroniclers knew their Latin too well. The vocabulary of Scott's novels had not yet led astray the makers of dictionaries, whether American or English. Nor were Irving's caricatures even dreamed of, though the English, who owe such a vast debt to the Dutch for their enrichment and civilization, were too foolishly ready to look down on all non-insulars and even Netherlanders as inferiors. Nor at that date were the northern provinces of the Republic spoken of as Holland — a misnomer that has outlived the name-giver, Napoleon.

The coming of these pioneer Walloons in 1624

was as the first drops of a shower followed by rills, yet uniting in one initial stream, which afterwards joined with vastly greater affluents, making the French Huguenot flood. The fact of French being the first language spoken in the homes of our four Middle States marks the beginning of American taste in dress, household furnishing, table equipment, personal adornment, and indulgence generally in æsthetic decoration, which differentiate us, in these details, even from standards that are fixed and notable in the British Isles.

The traveled American, visiting his ancestral home in England, is not long in perceiving this. Those of our sectional historians who keep up the legend of unmixed English culture and follow the notion that we are an English nation, do not see that the founding of homes in New York, by the Walloons, in 1624, was the protocol of a long school of education in tastes. This distinguished the American and his home from the British, even though language and innumerable inheritances come to us from the dear Mother Land of Britain — where dwelt the writer's known and recorded ancestors, in the records of the ninth century, and in England from the time of the Norman invasion. Nor is it realized by the general body of sectional writers that the fathers of our religious liberty are, with Roger Williams, Peter Minuit and William Penn, rather than either the Pilgrims or the Puritans of New England.

The Walloons made perceptible contributions to

the civilization that was to blend many strains into one. "Distinct as the billows, yet one as the sea," we might say of what was in the gift-laden hands of the French-speaking people. These came first from the Belgic Netherlands, then from Walloon France, and finally from nearly every one of the French provinces and from the lands of exile. They brought us many things for our enrichment in mental and economic resources and the improvement of our sensibilities.

On the finer side of life, their offerings are to this day manifest. In the colonial era, the interiors even of their frontier homes were neater and more attractive than those of the Dutch and English settlers. Instead of thick woolen, coarse cloth, or dowdy stuff at the windows, the glare of their "lights," whether of oiled parchment or greased paper, was tempered and mellowed with dainty white linen. On the floor, in place of sand and rushes, they spread textiles, made of odds and ends of worn-out or discarded clothing, or other dry goods. These, woven in their looms, made what we call rag carpet — cheerful to look at and pleasant for the feet to tread upon.

There was at first no need of rigid economy in larder or on the table, when game was abundant and flocks of wild pigeons darkened the sun. The forest was then their storehouse, and the garden their pantry, while they looked to the hills whence came their material help in herbs and simples. Afterwards, they introduced and showed the town-dwellers many

a delicious morsel, and even the delights of ox-
tail soup. The Newtown pippin, the quince and
grape culture, and the first vineyards were developed from what the French-speaking colonists
brought over. Apples, as a rule, were grafted on Indian stocks. In our generation, it is only the native
varieties of berries and fruit, or those budded on the
aboriginal stalks or trunks, that have survived, or
improved with the centuries. Nevertheless, while
all were men of their time, the wilderness, the frontier, and savage humanity had their influences upon
them; and these were early efficient in making one
new type of man, who could not be in full conformity
with Old World ideas, mental scope, or contemporary environment. One can love dear Mother England and her people and his own English ancestors,
without being afraid of either the facts or the truth
concerning others than British Islesmen who helped
to make the American composite. One can do this,
while detesting the European inheritances that still
linger from barbarism. Our forefathers were glad to
get rid of these, nor would have them in their new
home. In a word, the better England, the better
France, the better Belgium survived in America,
and the history of the United States rightly interpreted sheds glory on the old mother lands.

It needs no creative imagination to picture the
routine of life, on the ship of these initial home-
makers of our Middle States or in their new homes.
Daily prayer, the singing of Marot's psalms, and

the training of the children in the first principles of pure religion and morality, through the study of the Catechism and the Creed (the Twelve Articles of the Christian Faith), formed the routine of the months at sea. Those who, like the writer, have lived among the descendants of the Walloons, knowing them as intimate friends, as church officers, as leaders in business and society, and sharing their faith, inheritances, traditions, and ceremonies, can at least enter into the spirit, while comprehending the form of their life at home, on shipboard, and in the wilderness.

CHAPTER XVII

GOVERNOR PETER MINUIT

At whatever date Manhattan was settled with families, we know that Pierre Minuit, the Walloon, was the first governor duly commissioned as such, in the long and illustrious line of the executives in the Empire State.

He was most probably one of those men who loved his little joke. He often wrote his name phonetically, to help people of six nations, Belgic, French, German, Dutch, English, and Swedish, to learn his other name besides Pierre, Pieter, Petrus, or Peter. Those who knew no French had to be told how to pronounce his name properly — not with the final and hard dental, but with that "phonetic decay" in which a Frenchman revels. Even his autographs are found written Menuet, Minnuet, Minnewit, Minnewitz, and Minnawee.

This was like the Pilgrim Fathers, who, when in the Netherlands, signed their names in Hollandish, which was done to help the clerks and business men, who thought that English was only "broken Dutch." His real name, which was Peter Minuit, may be read any morning, as one walks down Fifth Avenue past the northwest corner of Twenty-ninth Street, where stands the fourth edifice of the church of 1628, in which he was an elder. There, also, is the bell which later called the worshipers to service in structures which have been successively wood, brick, and marble. In these edifices, the first a horse mill, have gathered for worship during many generations the members of the first fully organized church in North America. It began on Manhattan, and under the Walloon governor's administration.

Who was Peter Minuit?

His father was pastor of a Walloon church at Wesel, on the Rhine, about thirty miles east of the Dutch frontier. To this city of refuge gathered many hundreds of Belgic folk, who had fled when Alva's invaders entered their home land—all "orthodox" and also "Christians" — sent to hunt heretics. Successive waves of refugees found calm in Wesel, which of old was in the frontier of civilization and which has had a wonderful history. It was from this place that Charlemagne started upon his campaigns against those pagan Saxons whom we of to-day idealize almost to transfiguration.

The church built in the twelfth century in honor of St. Willibrod, the great apostle to the Germans, who had died A.D. 738, stood in this city.

In 1555, when the structure had become by age "a ruin under a roof," the English exiles, fleeing from Bloody Mary's persecution, arrived at Wesel. Within the ancient walls, a baby boy of the pilgrim father and mother, Willoughby d'Eresby and Catherine, Duchess of Suffolk, was born. A pilgrim and a stranger like his parents, he was here baptized. He

164

was christened and named, as was the White baby of the Mayflower, Peregrine, or pilgrim, his added name being Bertie. Many English exiles christened their infants with this name, Peregrine. Others, like Moses, named a son Gershom, that is, driven out, in token of their expulsion from their native land.

Shortly after this date, but more numerously from 1567, the Belgic Netherlanders flocked into the Duchy of Cleves and the city of Wesel. Stripped of their goods, many found domicile within the walls of the old church. To the pastor of these refugees was born a son, Pierre or Peter, the future governor of Nova Belgica.

Five items of glad news, one after another, cheered these lonely exiles. In 1609, Henry Hudson returned from his discovery of an unoccupied and lovely virgin land beyond sea. It lay between the two rivers which we call the Delaware and the Hudson. In 1613 this new, or eighth, province of the Dutch Republic received its geographical name, New Netherland. In 1619, the Dutch Union cause triumphed. In 1621, the West India Company, for the colonization of America, was formed. In 1623, Jesse de Forest and his company from Leyden were to be given free passage to the new land, which two years later, in 1626, was to have a civil government and be named (Terra) Nova Belgica.

Until 1664, many Walloons left Wesel for America by way of Rotterdam. This Rhine region became later the scene of war in which an English army took part. While the Mayflower was on her ocean way, Sir Horace Vere with his brave soldiers, acting with the German allies, was holding the Spaniards at bay; as usual, the Walloons and Huguenots suffered and were again scattered. During the Thirty Years' War, thousands of these doubly exiled Walloons fled into the Dutch Republic, some to remain, but many to cross the Atlantic.

Later on, in 1688, Louis XIV, infuriated because Germany gave shelter to the Huguenots, whom his minions had hunted out like vermin and driven from their home land, sent his armies to ravage this Rhine region called the Palatinate. This they did, exactly as did the Germans in France and Belgium, from 1914 to 1918. One war usually breeds another. Invaded nations have long memories.

On December 19, 1625, the ship named the Little Sea Mew, having on board Governor Minuit and his secretary, Isaac de Rasieres, with the new province's seal denoting that New Netherland was organized with a civil government under the name of Nova Belgica, started from the Weeper's Tower in Amsterdam to pass northward through the Texel. The people from this island, when at home named the Van Texels, were in America called the Van Tassels — as all who have read Washington Irving's romances may know, and as the honored names in the Tarrytown church records show.

Yet the governor's patience was sorely tried, for

he and his were kept a month in the Zuyder Zee because of the ice. No doubt sailors and passengers whiled away part of the time with their skates, sleds, ice yachts, and various winter sports; all of which, besides having Dutch names, were introduced into New Netherland and are with us to-day in New York and New Jersey. Minuit's title was Director-General of New Netherland. He arrived May 4, 1626.

The threefold functions of government, as differentiated by Isaiah (XXXIII. 22) first, and Aristotle after him, into executive, legislative, and judicial, were not yet formulated in the new colony, but in Nova Belgica, Minuit had to act in all three capacities. Not yet was evolved that wonderful system of checks and balances which, in the government of the United States, makes the complex political machinery work so well. Associated with the governor were also a council, a schout-fischal, or treasurer, and the secretary, Isaac de Rasieres.

The oldest known documents in the archives of the Empire and Keystone States, are those which record that in the first instance a Walloon, and in the second, the son of a Dutch mother, made treaties of peace with the Indians and paid for the land which they and their people were to occupy. There is the bill of sale of Manhattan, which, with the sufficing brevity of a telegram, yet with sufficient details, tells the double story. Yet this purchase of land on Manhattan was not understood by the Indians to

THE STORY OF THE WALLOONS

cover the entire island,[1] nor did it mark "the birth
of New York City." The transaction was a prelimi-
nary for all New Netherland. From this time forth,
settlers obtained valid land titles.

The ship returning to Patria carried good news
from the island and also from "up the river," showing that Mother Earth had done her part in making
the wilderness bloom and in providing food for man;
while in the homes the cradles rocked with new
treasures, when the first babies, a boy and a girl, began what was for each of them a long life voyage.
"Corn" in those very early days did not mean
maize — then called in Europe, where it was a curi-
osity, "Turkish wheat." In truth, it took some time
for the white man to learn from the natives the fine
art of its cultivation, its proper culinary preparation, and the gustatory delights, consequent upon
its correct treatment, by roasting, boiling, or mixing
with beans in succotash, which even yet Europe
scarcely knows. In Britain, without our hot American summers, Indian corn scarcely reaches the
height of a yardstick, by October. In Nova Belgica,
rye, barley, oats, buckwheat, canary seed, and beans
well supplied the larder for man, fowl, and beast, in
preparation for winter's needs.

Among the live things of glory and beauty, awakening sweet memories of the old home, was the blue
flax flower. Of the glossy silk-like fiber in the stalk,
the women soon began to make linen and much

[1] See Riker's *History of Harlem* for full proof of this.

168

later, carpet, lace, and tapestry. Even in these early days, the Walloons excelled the Dutch and English in the daintiness of indoor furnishing.

No mythical and few genuine articles of furniture, brought over on the early ships from the Netherlands, were seen, for example, in the famous loan exhibition in Schenectady in 1880; but dainty products in lace and linen, made even in early frontier days by the pioneer Walloons, were in trustworthy evidence. Of cake moulds and things smaller in bulk and easily portable, however, there were many.

The terse document which tells of the purchase of Manhattan states also that, besides what the vegetable world furnished, the animals that paid tribute for man's clothing, in a way that was to fill the coffers of the home land directors and the pockets of the merchants, served for barter. Even before this date, the beaver's effigy had entered heraldry as a welcome newcomer and was on the seal of Nova Belgica. For a century afterward, this animal, representing both value and the production of value, was the symbol and the standard of currency, the actual pelt serving in place of coin. It was fitting that the settlement on the frontier of the colony at the head of river navigation, where Albany now stands, should be named "Beverwijk" (Beverwyck).

Governor Minuit did not wait long before attending to the courtesies proper among Christians. He wrote a letter to Plymouth and closed with expression of sincere piety, commending to God's grace and favor the "High and Mighty Lords" of the Company, using the "complimental titles" of which Bradford tells us.

If monarchs boasted of their power in high-sounding terms of praise and in self-glorification, why should not republicans do the same? In the attributes and customs of autocracy or royalty, in whatever was worth imitating, the Dutch asserted equality by trumpet, flag, costume, badge of office, and in rhetoric, document, and fact. Hence their titles! Especially when on land and sea they had humbled Spain, and even by colonizing the continent claimed by His Most Christian Majesty — who so delighted in roasting his subjects — did the Dutch "put on airs." Most fittingly, also, did their legislators call themselves "Their High Mightinesses."

Among the most assuring items of news in the manifest of this initial ship, outward bound from what is now the world's greatest port and freighted with the first official document from New Netherland, was the report of the friendliness of the Indians — harbinger of the success of the Walloon venture. This was the dayspring of the full glory of possession by the Empire State of the largest store in America of wampum belts, seals, and signs of justice to the Indian and the perpetuity of his friendship.

Nearly two centuries after the schout-fischal had appraised, in guilders, with perhaps stivers and cents thrown in, the market value of the Manhattan of

GOVERNOR PETER MINUIT

1624, in his report to "John Company," Alexander Hamilton continued Peter Minuit's work. This descendant of Huguenots and America's greatest architect of government, adopted for Americans, in the States gathered in a federal republic (*e pluribus unum*), their financial system. Under the old Dutch flag, with six more stripes, and stars thirteen added, Hamilton gave us what was essentially the Dutch decimal system, with dalers (dollars), cents, and mills.

The old Teutonic arrangement of pounds, shillings, and denarii (£ s. d.) — which system meant varying standards of value in the different colonies — was rejected. A simpler arrangement, virtually that of the Netherlands, was adopted, though the Spanish symbol for dollars — the gates of Hercules ($) — was retained. Even in the writer's boyhood, the Spanish coins, the "two-pillared" silver dollar, the "levy" (eleven cents), and the "fip" (fivepence), were in general circulation. The guilder is now equal to four dimes, or eight nickels, or forty American cents.

Evidently Minuit was a man of energy, who desired to "do justice, love mercy, and walk humbly with God"; but he had enemies who slandered him; for the love of money was strong among the adventurers who began to flock in. Minuit's idea was to discover and develop to the full the resources of the new land. He found unusually large and fine timber in the region of the Mohawk, and so, utilizing some of the ship carpenters — probably fellow believers from Sweden, though all men from lands north of the Netherlands were called "Normans" by the Dutch — he built one of the largest seaworthy vessels of the time. It was pierced to carry thirty guns, for trading and fighting usually went together in those days. It crossed the ocean — being probably the first "liner" from America and from the Netherlands — and after exciting wonder for its size and excellent structure, was long used for trade in the West Indies.

The home directors, however, complained that this ship cost too much, which meant most probably that they wanted "quick returns"; that is, more revenue from the fur trade and easy money in their pockets. In fact, they were not very anxious that the colonists should be too enterprising, lest they might develop ambition to trade on their own account.

Minuit was too much of "a people's man" to suit a corporation, the first and last idea of which was "dividends." The non-stockholders who were not direct agents of the home corporation were supposed never to trade, but only to serve and till the soil. Like many capitalists in our time, "John Company" and the patroons were generous in providing for the colonists' comfort, thus aiming to secure good working and richly productive animals; but, from measures for the making and development of manhood and noble citizenship, they preferred to be excused.

All evidence seems to show that the same greedy men, of the same type of mind, with the "get-rich-quick" spirit, dominated the factions in the Dutch West India Company as prevailed also in the English corporation which had equipped the Mayflower, but also virtually fettered if they did not enslave the Pilgrims, while putting a veto on Robinson's ever reaching America. "Nature takes out of the man what she puts into the chest." In due time the Dutch West India went to financial smash.

The same data of information seem to prove that Governor Minuit was more earnest for justice to be meted out to the settlers than in currying favor with the corporation. At any rate, nepotism prevailed in the Amsterdam office. Minuit was recalled, and a Director's nephew, a clerk from one of the Company's desks, was put in his place. In hostile tradition, he stands without much character, brains, or experience, but with an excessive love and capacity for liquor. Wouter Van Twiller, who was sent in the place of the competent governor Minuit, furnished Washington Irving a fitting figure for his caricatures. Nevertheless, except when and where shackled by the Company's strict orders, Van Twiller was full of youth, fire, and energy in his acts. Until the new Director-General arrived, Sebastian Krol (pronounced *krull*), church elder, from whom the toothsome "cruller" — so tradition avers — took its name, had charge of affairs. In the years after 1664, the Directors-General of New Netherland were called by the English "Governors."

On reaching Europe and knowing that many of his

industrious and enterprising fellow Walloons were in
Sweden, Peter Minuit sought and was offered service
by Oxenstierna, the great Swedish Chancellor of Gustavus Adolphus, who directed the policy of Sweden
during the Thirty Years' War, and who was then in
the Dutch Republic. At his instigation, Minuit led a
colony of Swedes and Finns into the Delaware valley. The world knows their history and the Luther-
ans and Episcopalians their church life, while many
of the names in the Philadelphia and Wilmington
city directories still recall those of Scandinavian ancestors. Their church edifices, yet standing on the
historic spots, from which the large part of the two
cities have grown away, bear witness to the piety,
taste, and prosperity of these Swedes, Finns, and
Walloons.

It was to the glorious old church edifice, new in
1700 but now much altered in form, standing in the
leafy and woody Indian village of Wecaco, in the
southern part of the City of Brotherly Love, where
the singing birds were so plentiful, that Longfellow,
our poet of Huguenot descent, tells us Evangeline
came. In the once octagonal brick church of Gloria
Dei — which the writer as a child often attended,
part of his infancy and early childhood being spent
in Swanson Street on land purchased of a Swede of
that name, by William Penn — the beautiful ritual
of the Book of Common Prayer is still read on Sabbath days.

The world still waits for the poet, the painter, and

the sculptor to interpret in terms of art the story of both the Swedes and the Walloons.

When in Nova Belgica, during his six years' administration Peter Minuit, by his spirit and through his inheritances, showed himself a lover of freedom and more in sympathy with human beings than with soulless corporations. He was disgusted with the grasping spirit of the monopolists at home and of those greedy seizers of land in the colony, whom he often checkmated. He was so much of a people's man, that he was dismissed because of his too great sympathy with his fellow Christians and the colonists in general. He protected them as far as possible against unscrupulous men in "big business."

This son of a Huguenot minister was the precursor of another minister's son, a later champion of the lower classes, Jacob Leisler, who appeared in history when most sorely needed. Against the spirit of feudalism, both Dutch and English, that hindered the normal growth of New Netherland and New York, it was well for future America that she had two such men, who were, like Lincoln, assertors of the rights of the plain people, whom "God must have loved, because He made so many of them."

CHAPTER XVIII

SECRETARY ISAAC DE RASIERES

THERE are men and women who make their names famous in history by doing one thing. In the Bible there are many single-line biographies. They may write a poem, paint a picture, say a grand word, do a good act, or in a sentence reveal some short cut to knowledge. Perhaps at the time they may think that they are acting only in commonplace routine, doing nothing out of the ordinary program of each day's work. They might even "blush to find it fame." The results, of which the world takes notice, may be unknown to them, or follow long after they have passed away. They come to honor and know it not. After centuries of oblivion, a grateful people may summon genius to glorify their names, in painting, statue, memorial, or tablet. In the world's Hall of Fame are many Marys of low degree and Josephs raised from the pit. "History is a resurrection."

Such undoubtedly was the feeling of many of the Pilgrim Fathers. Neither they nor the Mothers knew anything of "the trumpet that sings of fame." Of the Unknown Soldier, who died in the Great War, we may say this also, as over his dust, "in the grave's democracy," kings bow their heads and salute him as one of those of whom the poet sings:

"On Fame's eternal camping-ground
Their snow-white tents are spread."

176

SECRETARY ISAAC DE RASIERES

One of such, among the Walloon pioneers in New Belgic Land, was the secretary of its first governor. He served well his chief and his masters in the West India Company. In addition to routine duties, he made a visit to old friends and neighbors in Leyden, the English Separatists at Plymouth, Massachusetts, to bear the Christian greetings of the governor of Nova Belgica and his fellow colonists of like faith and hope.

The letter of Isaac de Rasieres, written in 1628, to his friend and well-wisher, Samuel Blommaert, who lived in Amsterdam, gives what no other writing of the time has done; that is, a detailed picture of the social and Sabbath life of the Pilgrims at Plymouth. Incidentally, it reveals to us why, in America, the man in church still sits at the end of the pew nearest the aisle, in which, during colonial days, muskets were stacked for quick use in case of Indian attack. De Rasieres' painting in ink and words is as minute and fascinating as that in oil and on canvas of the Flemish artist Ostade, for it is full of lively details. His account of the church parade, led by Elder Brewster and Miles Standish, stirs us like a bugle blast, or the beat of drums. From de Rasieres' description George H. Boughton painted his famous picture.

To Governor Peter Minuit's letter Governor Bradford replied with equal courtesy and in the spirit of Christian brotherhood, writing in both Dutch and English.

THE STORY OF THE WALLOONS

De Rasieres penned his letter on the 26th of September, 1626, outside Fort Amsterdam, on Manhattan, in Nova Belgica, and in what some called New Avesnes, or New Avennes, on the plantation of Old Jan Lampo and Cornelis Van Voorst. It was north of Canal Street, where now stand lofty skyscrapers and edifices of steel and stone. We must remember that it was "Fort Amsterdam" first, instead of New Amsterdam, in Nova Belgica, and that America's mighty metropolis is an evolution from a fortress. In February, 1653, the village became the city of New Amsterdam.

The name "New Amsterdam," as the seal shows, was not in common use until 1654. The Walloons often spoke of the Manhattan settlement as "New Avesnes." De Rasieres' letter, giving us his first impression of the new Dutch province, its landmarks, its waters, its general features, its men and women, native and immigrant, is wonderfully vivid.

The Walloon secretary's second visit to Plymouth resulted in the introduction to New England of wampum, or Indian shell currency. This gave the English settlers a tremendous pecuniary advantage, helping them, by making trade more brisk and facile, to pay off their debts and gain financial independence. In the English colonies, wampum became the standard of value and of exchange, remaining so during more than a century.

De Rasieres' letter lay in the national archives at The Hague, until Dr. Eckhof of Leyden found, retranslated, and published it, in 1919, and wrote a biography of the prosperous secretary, who used French and Dutch equally well.

What were the chief events in the life of de Rasieres? We know that in 1628 he was too fat to be fond of a long walk, as Bradford tells us. From the great "Dutch Biographical Dictionary," vol. V, published in December, 1921, we learn that de Rasieres was born a day or two before October 15, 1595, at Middelburg, and was baptized in the Reformed Church. He was therefore four years younger than Bradford, who, even more than his Manhattan correspondent and visitor, had reason to remember this city, the "old home of freedom," — and of many Walloon refugees — as is told about in "The Young People's History of the Pilgrims." Quite possibly de Rasieres used to know Bradford, the Pilgrim historian, at Leyden, as well as in Massachusetts. The secretary's father was Laurens de Rasieres, most probably a Belgic refugee, and the way of his fortune was in the sea. On July 7, 1618, Isaac's brother Abraham was supercargo of the ship Sea Wolf.

Isaac, the boy, lost his mother, and in 1605 his father married again, taking as his bride Anna l'Hermite, of Antwerp, daughter of a Walloon mercantile family. When, in 1624, Isaac was thirty years old and then unmarried, he was appointed Secretary of Nova Belgica. He sailed in the ship Arms of Amsterdam (Het Wapen van Amsterdam), and arrived in America July 26, 1625. He was present officially with Governor Minuit, on September 23, 1626, at the purchase of Manhattan.

According to the requirements of the West India Company's charter, which definitely stipulated that the natives must be paid for the land which any Dutch colony occupied, Manhattan — meaning a place between two rivers — was occupied with the good will of the natives. They were satisfied, not with coin, which had no meaning or value to the Indian, but with articles of use and adornment, such as knives and beads, of which they were delighted to get possession. Subsequent history also showed that in the minds of the natives the northern half, beyond the fort and farms, was not included in the sale, as is told, in detail, in Riker's admirable "History of Harlem."

Evidently Isaac made several voyages over the Atlantic to North and South America. He returned to Holland and in 1633 he courted and led to the altar in marriage, Eva Bartels, a young lady twenty-four years of age, niece of the Walloon Jean Raye, one of the West India Company's officers. The wedding was in the French or Walloon church, and registry was duly made for the city archives.

On this occasion, as at all weddings in the Netherlands, there was gathered a collection for the poor. It was even a part of the covenant between man and wife, as set down in the ritual, as the writer knows, from long use of the Netherlands Marriage Form. A bride in the old or in the new Belgica hardly felt that she was married, unless she heard the coin jingle for others.

Not liking to serve under the blunderer, Wouter Van Twiller, "by merit raised to that bad eminence" of folly — the same of whom Washington Irving makes so much deserved fun — Mr. and Mrs. Isaac de Rasieres made "a hazard of new fortune" by going to Brazil, where her family was in the profitable sugar business. In those days, a Dutchman could get rich much more quickly in South, than in North America. Yet on the sea, business between the Netherlanders and the Portuguese was as much a matter of fighting as of trading. "Bills of exchange," in those days, were likely to be in the form of cannon balls; for the Iberian nations, to which a papal bull had given the two halves of the "heathen" world for an inheritance, still clung to the idea of the infallibility of the edicts issued from the city on the Tiber, at which the Dutch scoffed.

In South America sons were born to him. Laurens de Rasieres was named after the boy-baby's grandfather. He saw the light in 1636, was baptized April 19, but died in 1641. In 1639, a second son took his name, Isaac, from his father. To his third son was given the name of Laurens.

Prosperity followed the ex-secretary of Nova Belgica, for he owned three sugar mills, to which he gave the names "Amstel," "Middelburg," and "the Rasieres." In 1651 and 1654 he was living in Holland, doubtless enjoying his fortune made in sugar.

Later, we find him visiting Barbados, in the West
Indies, and here his son Laurens married Aletta van
Hontum. Of this couple, bride and groom ("bei-
der," or both together), the portrait was painted, at
Brussels, by the great artist Nicholas Maes. The
family tradition is that Isaac was also governor of
Tabago, which is fifteen miles from the Panama
Canal zone. All this we know from Dr. Eckhof's
researches published in 1919.

With William Bradford and some wise men, we
believe that "letters are the best part of history."
Certainly, in place of the long speeches which
most ancient and some modern historians put in
the mouths of the characters described by them,
we should rather have from "all the hands that
wrought" the missives which they penned. Would
that there had been, in earliest colonial days, more
writers of what the French call in painting *genre*,
that is, not of history, landscape, theology, or economics, but of human incidents, events and affairs;
and that their penwork were still extant! Such
survivals would save us from many of the later mon-
strosities of partisanship, which both deface and
defile the fair visage of truth, in what is called
most unworthily "history." Nor would we so often
read into the records of centuries ago the ideas current in our own times.

CHAPTER XIX

FOOD FOR THE SOUL

IN Nova Belgica, though their feet were set on the new continent, the Walloon Christians at first had no church of their own. Yet there was daily food for the soul, in family worship, instruction in the catechism, prayer and song in the household, for in their faith they laid emphasis on religion in the home. The very essence of the Calvinistic form of religion lies in instruction and actual experience. As in chemistry the "nascent" moment of the release of an element is the most potent, so is it also in church history. Catechizing means teaching, by word of mouth, through question and answer, the great truths of faith and duty, in a simple form suitable for young people.

So also to-day, the missionary of Reformed religion, in teaching the good news of God — the message of love from our Father in Heaven — begins at once to translate the Bible into the language of the people, thus making both allegiance to the Founder and the active exercise of faith and reason a supreme duty and a joy. In other forms of propagation, the method is by pictures, crosses, medals, or other symbols, while allegiance to the Church is insisted upon as peremptory and supreme. The former process goes to the roots of life and rebuilds a nation. On the

183

"foreign" field, the second method does not greatly disturb the old order of things. It is the religion of reality, more than of symbols, and even more than wars and bloodshed, trade and commerce, that has recreated Japan, China, and the other nations of Asia.

Such was the law and custom in the early primitive Church. When, however, religion became a system of symbols, ritual, autocracy and a political engine, with power centralized at one place, with one bishop, the catechizing or teaching of children was gradually and in large measure given up, the rite of confirmation taking its place. Instead of brotherhood, democracy, and personal inward experience, there were imposed the outward clamps of authority.

In other words, the power of the individual and the family was taken away and put into the hands of a caste, or corporation, which could control all human life, from the cradle to the grave. The old apostolic declarations, "ye are a royal priesthood," and that the "elders" of the church at Ephesus were also "bishops," were ignored. Instead of systematic, intelligent moral training, there were confirmations, and instead of an inward change, pretty dresses, chaplets of flowers, "first communion" celebrations by children in only "one kind," that is, bread soaked in wine, which was given from the hands of a priest, in place of, as in earlier days — before the clerical caste was formed — all being equal at one table. These were but a few of the many changes from

TABLET ON THE LAW SCHOOL OF NEW YORK UNIVERSITY, WASH-
INGTON SQUARE, NEW YORK, IN HONOR OF THE DUTCH AND
WALLOON TEACHERS IN NOVA BELGICA, OR NEW NETHERLAND
Erected, 1909

early Christianity, which the Reformed thought unwarrantable.

All Christian catechisms are and must be based, first of all, upon the Ten Commandments — the moral law; the Lord's Prayer — center of all devotions; and then, more or less, on the so-called "Apostles' Creed"; or, as the Walloons and Dutch called it, "The Twelve Articles of the Christian Faith." This last is theology, that is, the adjustment of what men know to what they believe; or, in the many changes of meaning which words undergo, the harmony of what men believe with what they say they know, or at least apprehend.

Of all catechisms made at the time of the Reformation, or later, that of Luther is the simplest and best fitted for a child. Yet it has the grave defect of following the Roman plan of omitting the second commandment and splitting the tenth into two parts. Instead of the phrase "The Holy Catholic Church" is substituted "The Holy Christian Church."

Calvin's catechism is fuller and more logical than Luther's, but is not so well fitted for the minds of children. Hence, in time, it was superseded by the Heidelberg and Westminster Catechisms and other forms of statements of Christian belief, put in question and answer. Yet for a long time Calvin's catechism was the only one used in the Walloon churches. In fact, this was decided upon at the Synod of Wesel in 1568. At the very time when the Spaniard in the Netherlands was imitating the

Turk, in his method of propagating religion by fire
and sword, the Reformed Walloons at Wesel made
choice of both the gospel and the method of the
Founder; that is, by spiritual instruction. This also
meant reality in place of symbols; or, personal experience in the individual soul, instead of the mere
fiat of authority.

One notable fact is, that at the very beginning
of the Reformation, the great men and teachers
thought it worth while to devote their time, talents,
and care to the children and without regard to sex.
In this, Christianity differs, by a mighty contrast,
from the other great religions of the Buddha and of
Mahomet. One has only to read the Koran and
"The Sacred Books of the East," to see these
religions in action and to discern this clearly.
Among the oldest of Christian paintings in the catacombs of Rome is that of the Good Shepherd bearing a lamb on his shoulders. One of the initial hymns
of the Christian Church, as translated by Henry
M. Dexter, begins, "Shepherd of tender youth."

In the American wilderness, the Walloons, tired of
fighting wild beasts in the spiritual Ephesus of Europe, found nothing worse in their new environment.
For, until stirred up by political and religious hatred
emanating from French Canada, or maddened by
the white man's poisons or aggressions, the Indians
were friendly. Though Nature confronted them
with perils, she offered also allurements and rewards.

For "provisions to sustain the mind" and feed

their souls, they had their precentor, who led the song and who read sermons. The beautiful liturgy of the Reformed Church was used then, more than in later years, when the sermon occupied so large a place and so long a time in the service. There was also the Visitor, or Comforter of the Sick, who came with consolation to the needy with the passages of scripture already selected — a form of service originally prepared by Caspar van der Heyden, at the Synod of Embden in 1571. It was this form of consolation that the great John of Barneveldt had read to him, just before being led to execution, declaring that in this confession of faith he was willing to die.

At every morning worship, the Ten Commandments were read either by the Lector or by the pastor, and usually commented upon. There was no idea in the Huguenot mind of formality, mere routine, or custom in partaking of holy communion. There must be preparation and searching of heart, as to whether the guests at the Lord's Table, besides "being received in mercy," were accounted "worthy partakers of this heavenly meat and drink." In a word, the preponderant idea was ethical and spiritual, rather than mere adherence to church rules.

Yet on the whole, as centuries slipped by and persecution was but a memory, the tendency in the Reformed churches was from the old "congregationality" to "ministeriality." The Domine attained a

disproportionate importance, while the individual
church member was too much inclined to excuse
himself and let the parson do the work. In time, the
reformed needed reforming, for the springs dried
up, and, on "the principle of the crust," religious life
became too much an outward matter of routine. So
forth came the "Quakers," the "Methodists," the
"New Lights," and others, whose stigma was, in the
end, glorious, and whose nicknames turned to titles
of honor.

The pioneer Walloons in Nova Belgica did not
have to wait many years for a pastor. When he
came, in 1628, the first completely organized church
in America took its being on Manhattan. The Domine, that is, a pastor with authority, not a "dominie" — which is a Scotch title, meaning a schoolmaster — was the Reverend Jonas Michælius. Born in
1577, he was a graduate of Leyden University, in the
class that matriculated September 6, 1600. At least
the name of Joannes Michælius is in the list for that
year. It is most probable that in his college days
he knew, in Leyden, some of those Walloons who
later, in 1623, emigrated to America. Michælius
married in 1612. After Christian work in the Dutch
colony in Brazil, he returned to Holland in 1627.
Entering the service of the West India Company,
he sailed out of the Texel, with his wife and three
children, for America.

The two letters of Michælius sent home from
Manhattan are among the most graphic and de-

tailed sources of authority for the earliest history of the pioneers and founders of the Empire State. After seven weeks in their new American home, his children were left motherless by the decease of his wife, in June, 1628. How pathetic those first graves of Christian exiles at Plymouth and on Manhattan!

Michælius formed inside the fort the mother church, which is now housed in two edifices, the one on Fifth Avenue at Twenty-ninth Street and the other at Forty-seventh Street, with many daughters all united under one Collegiate body, or Consistory. Fifty communicants sat down to the Eucharist, and Michælius read the tender and beautiful words of the "Form Preparatory to the Lord's Supper," which came from the pen of John Calvin. In the congregation were many Walloons, and the two church elders in the Consistory were Governor Peter Minuit and Jan Huyghens, both refugees from Wesel. As only certain ones of the older Walloons could speak or understand a formal discourse in Dutch, the Domine preached also in French, writing out his sermons in that language, so as to be exact in pronunciation and style. For centuries a majority of Dutch domines spoke more than one language and read several of them.

In 1628, this widower went back in the ship Eendraght (Unity) to Patria, as the home land was called, for the education of his daughters. The Dutch Republic then led the world in the education of women, for the elementary schools sustained by taxation were open to girls, as well as boys, as were also the schools in New Netherland — which colony was the pioneer in the United States as champion of the education of women. The records in Albany show that probably seventy-five per cent of the Netherlands women could write their own names, which was far from being the case in the other colonies. The biography of Michælius, so far as it is known, that is, to the year 1638, is given by Dr. Eckhof, in the great "National Dutch Dictionary of Biography" now in course of publication. His record ends with the year 1638, for the archives of the town, in which he later lived, perished some years ago in fire.

Serving the twenty-nine Reformed churches in New Netherland, from 1628 to 1700, were thirty-three ministers, most of them Dutch, the large majority being graduates of universities and able to preach in French. Of the total number, however, at least a half dozen were, by birth, Walloons, or, later, from France. Four of them officiated regularly in that language, going from church to church, as their services were needed; especially on Manhattan, Staten and Long Islands, and at Esopus, New Paltz, Wiltwick, Rondout, Schenectady, Kingston, and New Rochelle.

Several of the domines were learned in one or more of the Indian dialects, both Iroquois and Algonquin, and did noble Christian work among the savages, in some cases gathering the Indian children into classes. In the records of the church on the frontier, at Schenectady, the writer counted up the names of about one hundred and fifteen Indian pupils or converts.

CHAPTER XX
RICH FARMS ON MANHATTAN

FROM the Dutch map of Manhattan by Vingboom, 1624–39, translated and annotated by Mr. Dingman Versteeg and compiled and published by Mr. Edward Van Winkel, in 1916, we get a glimpse of the prosperity of the Walloons on Manhattan

From the first a distinction was made between a "bouwèrie" or farm (i.e., improved land, with buildings) and a "plantation." On the rough land, even while still virgin forest, one could raise corn and tobacco, the latter being one of the first gifts made to the Nova Belgicans by the Pilgrims of Plymouth.

For the grain, fruit, and vegetables brought from Europe, more carefully tilled land, even that ploughed and harrowed, was necessary, It was possible to go into the woods, plant corn or tobacco in the shade, and then, by "girdling" the trees, to make the leaves quickly wilt. This let in enough sunshine to ripen the maize during the hot summer. Such a "clearing" or "slashing" was a plantation. The fields under cultivation made farms. In like manner, a new settlement, in its beginning, when men lived in bark houses, was a "concentration," but a' more mature collection of people with houses was a "colony."

Bouwerie No. 1 was occupied by Governor Minuit, when the colony consisted of but two hundred souls. His survey showed that the island was about twenty-two hundred acres in area. His imposing house was on Deutel Kill (wedge, or bung creek) near the East River. This one, with a score or more of "kills," or streams, has long ago been filled up. Quite early, but more generally by the English after 1664, the distinction was made between "Manhattan Island" and "the Island of Manhattan," as two districts, divided by a stream long since canalized first, and then forgotten.

Bouwerie No. 3 was occupied by the Walloon, Gerrit Theusz de Reux (de Reus). Engaged as a farmer by Kilian Van Rensselaer, he had come over with four laborers in the ship Salt Mountain, to establish a farm on Blommaert's Kill, on de Laet's Island (near Albany) June 15, 1632. This island was named after the great editor and historian John de Laet, whose daughter and a son-in-law were at Beverwyck, or Rensselaerwick. As a justice of the peace, de Reus was presented by Van Rensselaer, the patroon, with a black hat having a silver band. During his absence from Manhattan, the farm was managed by another Walloon, Jehan Ides. De Reus returned to Holland in 1634 and died in 1639.

The first schout for Van Rensselaer was Rutger Hendrixsen van Soest, who was presented with a silver-plated rapier, with a baldric and a black hat with a plume, his station being one official step higher than that of de Reux.

The plantation of Jan Lampo, who was schout-fischal — "a sort of attorney-general" — who came from Cautel in Auvergne, France, was on Farm No. 8. For three years Isaac de Rasieres lived with him.

10. Governor Wouter Van Twiller, who arrived in April, 1633, had a tobacco farm. His house was probably the first erected north of Canal Street.

12. This was the plantation of another Walloon, Mr. Lesle de Neve Sinx.

Farm No. 19, of about two hundred acres, was owned by Loen Ontangle (Jean de la Montayne) born in Leyden and a student in the university there, husband of Rachel de Forest, the daughter of "the founder," Jesse de Forest. Originally called Muscoota, this piece of land was chosen by Henry de Forest, in April, 1637, in a grant from Wouter Van Twiller. It lay "between the hills and the kill," that is, from Morningside Heights to Harlem Creek, which rose near Mount Morris Park and emptied into the Harlem River. The northern boundary was at 124th Street and the southern at 109th Street. Henry de Forest died childless, July 26, 1637, and de la Montayne completed the buildings. The spring on this farm, still living and flowing, was long known as Montayne's Fountain, and the bouwerie was called Vredendal, or Peacedale. In Riker's "History of Harlem" and in Mrs. de Forest's "A Walloon Family in America," we have pretty full descriptions of this part of Manhattan.

37 and 38. Vingboom, the map-maker, accredits

four plantations to "Gegoergesyn." On June 16, 1637, Joris Jansen Rapalje, who had first, in 1628, settled on the site of Albany, obtained a patent for his farm at the Wallabout in Brooklyn. His baby Sara, born June 9, 1625, was the first Christian daughter born in New Netherland — according to her declaration, on April 4, 1656. To-day the East Brooklyn Savings Bank in Brooklyn occupies the site.

The horse mill inside the fort, in the upper story of which divine worship was held on Sundays, was built in 1627, by the Walloon, François Molemaecher. The old millstones are still preserved and have been photographed by a descendant of Krol, the famous all-around worthy. This lover of true history, Mr. William Brewer, has reared also a fitting memorial in the Reformed Church on Second Avenue.

The larger grain or grist mill, outside the fort, finished in 1626, in the year of Minuit's arrival, stood on a knoll. To the settlers it must have been homelike to see its great sails fluttering and its arms revolving. As was the custom from time immemorial, the occasion of completion was one marked with ceremonies and good cheer. No doubt the sight of a windmill softened the smart of homesickness, for now the landscape began to look more like that of the old country; while the canal, soon to be dug and embanked, added to the pleasing illusion. The province of Holland and the place of the Walloons' last home was already famous for its artificial waterways, but Hainault in Belgic Land did not receive its net-work of canals until long after the Huguenot Wal-loons had left it, nor until hard fuel had been discov-ered beneath the ancient Coal Forest and utilized.

39. Claes Carstenz Norman had a farm on Long Island, just north of the Wallabout. In March, 1647, he received a patent for land on the west side of the Hudson River. With Dirck Jansen Dey, he was the first known settler of Bayonne in New Jersey, though the name of the city came from a later French Huguenot.

40. Dieryck the Norman, or Dirck Volkerson, had this farm in 1639. His house and lot were on Man-hattan, but he farmed on Long Island.

The frequency of the name or designation of a man as "Norman," "Dane," "Swede," "Norwe-gian," or "Scandinavian" in general recalls the po-litical situation of Europe. Largely through the ac-tivities of Gustavus Adolphus, in the Thirty Years' War, many natives of the northern countries, adven-turers, soldiers, etc., were in the Netherlands ready for a "hazard of new fortunes." Thousands of Wal-loons had fled to Denmark and Sweden and thence came to America, with the aid of the Dutch West India Company. Some of the most enterprising of the New Netherland and New England pioneers were Normans of Scandinavian descent.

Interesting documents show how liberally the Manhattanese were provided for, in the way of cat-tle, sheep, and horses — which were brought over first in 1625. The list of 1630 shows on the Minuit farm twenty-eight, in all, of mares, stallions, and cows, besides fourteen sheep. On that of Gerrit de Reux were twenty.

When the later ships of the West India Company came over, laden largely with Walloons, as well as with Flemings and Dutch folks, the reinforcement to farm and house life was notable. In the models and structures of the average house of fairly well-to-do people, those of the old country were followed. It is true that in many cases, one prolonged roof covered both the human habitation and that of the shelter for the cows. The animals yielding daily tribute of nourishment for men were treated in a measure as fellow beings, worthy of constant care, while the virtue which is next to godliness was supreme.

One notable feature, more common in feudal days, but made effective on the American frontier, was the "overhang" of the first story. By this, in case of Indian attack, the dwelling was made into a fort for the protection of the garrison. Those within could fire on their enemies below, or throw water upon the blazing arrow, or hay-laden cart, which, when captured from the barn by the savages, was set on fire and pushed up to the walls or door. Even in the writer's lifetime, many of these homely structures, thus equipped for efficient defense, were still standing in the Mohawk Valley.

Neither to glorify fact, nor to transfigure tradition, but to state reality, from study, sight, and ex-

197

perience — and who knows human nature better than the pastor? — the best gift brought to the making of the American nation was the character of these people, as mellowed by persecution and exile. The orator in the forum or preacher in the pulpit may be well acquainted with human nature from books, but the shepherd of a flock — not sitting at a confessional, but familiar with the welcome and atmosphere of homes — knows beating hearts and inner lives. In our earlier American life, Walloon and Huguenot may have been but as lumps in the cup; yet though the form is lost, the sweetness abides.

CHAPTER XXI
THE ISLAND OF THE STATES

WELL named and of happy omen were the two islands named "Staten" or the States — the one in North America and the other at the tip end of the continent on Tierra del Fuego. Both of them were first discerned and given place on the world's maps by daring explorers sent out by the free Republic, that had triumphed over the despotism of Spain — the one in 1609 by the discoverer of New York's noblest river; the other in 1615 by skipper William Cornelis Schouten, a native of Hoorn, in North Holland, and co-worker with the Walloon Lemaire.

Both these ships had been sent out by Europe's foremost men of science. Both represented the forces of a new age — the age of public schools, free printing-presses, a higher position for women, and the right of man to govern himself in soul as well as body. These ships were the embodiments afloat of the law and order of freedom, as against despotism. They were harbingers of a better era in the world's history. They sailed into a new age of human progress.

Both islands were named in honor of the federal union of seven states — prototype of the larger American Commonwealth beyond the Atlantic, that was to extend from ocean to ocean.

THE STORY OF THE WALLOONS

Hudson's ship, besides bearing in its name the token of victory and success, the silver Half Moon, foreshadowed, in the very composition of its crew, the union of two great peoples in the making of the future United States of America. The captain, mate, and one half of the sailors were English, the other half being Dutch. In the evolution of the American Commonwealth, which, until 1791, consisted of but thirteen States, the Britons and the Netherlanders led and wrought together, while the Northern, the Central, and the Southern colonies were becoming one organism.

Staten, the sentinel at the gateway of a continent, has been called Huguenot Island, because so many of these people, with consciences that were not in the market, made their homes on its soil. Not a few local names, to this day, are the outstanding proofs and telltale witnesses of occupation, first by the Belgic and later the French Huguenots.

Even from the initial ship, the New Netherland, of 1624, some Walloons began their fortunes here, but they were few and not long was their abiding on the island. The Indians seemed implacable, and on account of the red men's menace, the earliest white pioneers were summoned to the "concentration," as the term was, on Manhattan; though later, some came back to suffer yet again in tempting fortune.

Were we to tell in detail this island's history, we should truthfully picture to ourselves not one ship, of name and record, like the New Netherland, bearing the Walloons to America, but rather the catalogue of a fleet. These vessels, from 1624 even to the great occultation of their story by the more numerous Huguenots from France, came laden with eager refugees. These made homes, we know not how many, upon the flats and hills of the Island of the States. These Belgic Walloons of 1624 were pioneers and pilots of the French Huguenots who came numerously after 1685. They, like the Pilgrim Fathers, were forerunners of the larger (Puritan) immigration.

It is after the Revocation that the names of Chaillé, Duché Pintard, Chadaine, Bodine, Depew, Mersereau, Boudin, La Conte, Disosway, and scores of other families of the same speech and faith are found. Many of their descendants, bearing those honorable and honored patronymics, are still among us, doing the world's work. Not a few stand high on the rolls of fame. Among the inscriptions in the cemeteries, one can read of many more that in ability or achievement rose above the average commoner. On the church rolls, however, is the larger number preserved and recognizable.

There are also deserted and forgotten graveyards, in which the unnamed sleep. Too frequently, the lone private and family God's Acres have been ploughed over, and the dust of those once above ground rests under edifices, highways, or harvests. This is also true of Schenectady, where in the open space at the junction of streets with names of what

in the Middle Colonies were never politically joined
— "Church" and "State" — lie the unnamed.
Rightly did the latter thoroughfare, leading to Albany, long bear the name of the Street of the Martyrs, because the Dutch and Walloons, slaughtered
in the massacre of February 9, 1690, were the victims of sectarian hate at the hands of Frenchmen
and savages who served the despot Louis XIV. The
favor-seeking letter from the leader of the raid, descriptive of the massacre, was addressed to the mistress of Louis XIV, Madame de Maintenon.

Long did Schenectady in the North bear the name
of the "Dorp," or village; and so also was the first
settlement on Staten Island named — both being
suburban to a city. Thrice was the insular enterprise
destroyed by the Raritan Indians; yet on Staten Island is still the New Dorp, and here also is Huguenot Park. It was towards the end of the seventeenth century that Huguenots numerously settled
at Marshland, now Green Ridge.

Staten Island is rich in contacts with history, for
we read of Coleman's Point, where one of Hudson's
men in the Half Moon was slain by an Indian arrow.
Among the edifices, at this writing, still standing,
besides the Du Bois House, is the Groot House, of
Dutch architecture — the original Walloon family
being named Le Grand. With the Jacques house
were willows from St. Helena and boxwood from
Mount Vernon, while the fence is from the old home
in Whitehall Street, on Manhattan. The Mersereau

House and the Crocheron House has each its interesting tradition — the latter relating to the founder of the family. To escape execution in France, he hid in a hogshead on board a ship, in which were his neighbors bound for America. What wonderful tales, around their winter firesides, of flight and hiding and disguise and hairbreadth escapes, these pioneers could tell!

Still intact, or the foundations visible, are the former homes of the Perrines, Cortelyous, Cubberlys (Coverles), Guyons, Sequines, and Disosways. Thoreau, who taught school here, was of Huguenot ancestry. Though rich in the lore of the Indians, of the Italian and Dutch explorers, of the New Netherlanders of several strains, and of the Huguenots, Staten Island's later history does not now concern us.

Those who would, in their imaginations, reproduce its social and religious aspects must, besides the modern local histories, read the reports of the two Labadists of 1679. These tell of *le chaudronnier* (coppersmith) who had been a soldier in Brazil, and of old Pierre la Jardinière, who was threescore years and ten. By the year 1698, there were on the island seven hundred and twenty-seven persons, not a few of whom, thrice persecuted, had come as refugees from the Island of St. Kitts (St. Christopher) in the West Indies. The popish plots and brutal despotism of Louis XIV had cast long shadows across the Atlantic, and these kept people in America in constant fear of the French conquest of America and of being

chained in prison, or on benches of the floating purgatory of the galleys. No wonder then that they were
"Leislerians" almost to a man, and certainly to a
woman. After King William's accession to the British throne, their fears vanished. Almost as a matter
of course, these people who counted liberty of conscience as the best thing in life stood by their best
friend, Jacob Leisler.

What is characteristic of the entire Walloon immigration to America is true also of the Walloons and
later Huguenots from France who settled on Staten
Island. Their collective history is recoverable almost entirely from their church records. Their careers centered in the church. In their case it is impossible to divorce their story from their religion and
conscience. Without an organization at first, Domines Michælius and Drisius from the fort on Manhattan, and later Domine Selyns — beginner of the
literature of New York—visited them once a month.

For twenty years they had private worship, sacred
song, monthly preaching, and baptism of their children; but in 1680 a church with French services was
organized and an edifice at Stony Brook was built.
The Reverend David Bon Repos served as pastor,
having been called by the Dutch Church on Manhattan to minister exclusively to those who used
the French tongue.

Their second spiritual shepherd was the famous
Pierre Daillé — "full of fire, godliness, and learning," as his colleague, Domine Selyns, declared.

THE ISLAND OF THE STATES

Born in France in 1649, Daillé became at thirty professor of Christian theology at Saumur, in one of the four Huguenot seminaries in France. Under the bigotry of Louis XIV, these schools were broken up and their faculties banished. Arriving in America in 1683, Daillé proved himself a veritable apostle to his fellow countrymen, the scattered Huguenots. Besides being pastor of the French church in New York, we find him on Staten Island, at Harlem, New Paltz, Bushwick, Long Island, Hackensack, New Jersey, New Rochelle, several places on Long Island, and wherever there was the greatest need, comforting, cheering, and helping souls. Called to Boston, Daillé served the French Reformed Church on School Street, from 1696 to 1715, making a deep impress on the life of the city.

It was hard for the strictest Puritans to encourage, by granting toleration, in allowing among them such people of joyous temperament, who celebrated Christmas and Easter. These church festivals were unnoticed in Boston, until well into the nineteenth century. Yet Daillé won all hearts, and when dying too soon, at sixty-six, he was mourned by thousands.

On Manhattan, in 1688, the Huguenots left the old Dutch church in the fort and worshiped in the new edifice built on Marketfield Street. In the latter part of his ministry in New York, Daillé had a colleague, the Reverend Mr. Peiret, who served the churches from 1688 to 1704, preaching usually in the city, while Daillé itinerated in the country.

THE STORY OF THE WALLOONS

One need not here enlarge upon the history of the
Huguenot churches in America, nor on the antiquarian details — for which one may look in the local
histories. Their general spirit and procedure was
that of the Reformed Churches everywhere. In good
season, these people set a good example, for all time,
to immigrants. They quickly conformed in language
and ways of life to the country in which they dwelt.
Naturally, they coalesced first with the Dutch and
later with the American churches of the Episcopal or
the Presbyterian order, and through marriage helped
in forming the American Commonwealth.

Still another nationality was to be added to the
American composite when, on Christmas Day, 1656,
a company of hunted Christians from Piedmont,
Italy, the Waldenses, one hundred and sixty-seven in
number, sailed for New Netherland. They had been
driven out by the Duke of Savoy, who had joined
that company of rulers who, in the name of God,
while trying to kill conscience, proved themselves
unwittingly to be American colonizers. It was in
behalf of these people that Cromwell protested with
effect and Milton wrote his seraphic sonnet, beginning: "Avenge, O Lord, thy slaughtered saints."
The West India Company, in 1656, gave the Waldenses passage in the ships named Prince Maurice,
Bear, and Flower.

Let it be repeated that commonplace records
abundantly show that the Dutch Republic excelled
all other states of Europe in the welcome given to

the Pilgrim fathers, mothers, and children of all sorts, and to people of many nations, Hebrew and Christian. Even a pagan received Christian treatment. Not at once, but in time, the spirit of the Father of his Country, William the Silent, prevailed. Bradford, the typical Pilgrim Father, when still in England, heard, and when in Holland found it to be true, "that religion was free for all men" — a freedom which irritated the sectarian bigots and fanatics of every State Church, whether called Protestant or Catholic. None denounced this Republic for its tolerance more than the English State Churchmen. No name was too vile to bestow upon the country and people who held to the belief that "when persecution begins, Christianity ends."

Despite all human precautions for safety, disaster befell these Italian fugitives from the cruelty of man. Saved by the Dutch in Europe, they met in America distress from Nature. A terrible storm drove the three ships apart. Two of these, the Bear and the Flower, though delayed, got safely to Manhattan; but the larger one, the Prince Maurice, which had most of the Waldenses aboard, struck at midnight on the ice-bound coast of Long Island, near Fire Island. Through the dark and cold hours of a winter night, they waited until daybreak. Then the crew and passengers climbed over the ice to the shore, hoping to make a fire and get warm. But on landing they found only sand, with no fuel, even of driftwood, of grass, or of weeds. There they waited, shivering, and at a loss to know what to do; for at first no human beings were visible.

Yet for three centuries, on this wreck-strewn shore, have dwelt the Shinnecock Indians, sons of the soil. These human brothers of ours, down to our day, when but a handful of survivors remain, have ever been the helpers, friends, and rescuers of the shipwrecked, even at the hazard of their own lives. Theirs has been a permanent "Life Saving Institution."

At that critical winter hour, the Shinnecocks appeared and came to the help of the Waldenses. One of them carried a letter to Governor Stuyvesant, imploring his aid. At once the kindly old hero sent out yachts and soon went himself to help the distressed people. In a short time, all these Waldenses were on Manhattan, where they found their other friends from the two ships. Most of the cargo of the Prince Maurice was later salvaged, but for many years the sea-scoured and wave-whitened bones of the once gallant ship were visible — one of a hundred or more that have ended their careers on this ancient Island of Shells.

After a short stay, the majority of the Waldenses made settlement on the Delaware. Some chose Staten Island, to which, in 1662 and 1663, other Waldensian families came. It is from these facts that the names of Italian origin, found on Staten Island so early in the history of New York, are accounted for. From 1652 to about 1750, their chief settlement, so tradition avers, was at Stony Brook; after which, the Waldenses were lost in the mass of the American people.

At last, on the dial-plate of time, the day and the hour for the honoring of the founders of Staten Island drew near. In 1922, led by the generosity, zeal, skill, and taste of architect Ernest Flagg, the people of Huguenot Park moved in the enterprise of erecting a fitting monument to their Walloon and French ancestors, to be called the Huguenot Church, with a Memorial House to be for the good of the community. May this undertaking be but the harbinger of works of art, beauty, and usefulness that shall keep alive the memories of those to whom we, as Americans, owe so much.

CHAPTER XXII

THE AMERICAN PALATINATE

THE American who knows well the City of Brotherly Love, which was laid out by William Penn with the regularity of a chess board, having numbered streets crossed by others with forest-tree names, feels wonderfully at home in Mannheim, that is, "man's home" — on the Rhine. The question whether the founder of Pennsylvania borrowed his idea from ancient Babylon, or the Heavenly Jerusalem, that "lieth foursquare" and had a river flowing through it, or from Mannheim, is not here debated.

Penn traveled much in Reformed countries. From Crefeld, in Germany, and other towns and cities along the Rhine, he led large numbers of natives and refugees, the Mennonites in Friesland and notably the Welsh, his own countrymen, from other lands into the territory named by King Charles II "The Groves of Penn." Two of our poets, both of Huguenot blood, have sung the praises of Penn's "godly experiment."

Whittier celebrated the Mennonite Pastorius in "The Pennsylvania Pilgrim." Of the streets of the City of Brotherly Love named from the trees of the forest, "as if to appease the Dryads, whose haunts they had invaded," Longfellow, in his "Evangeline," tells us. One of the first duties of Penn, shortly after

210

his arrival, was to naturalize a company of Walloons — very probably from Belgic Land, by way of Germany and Holland. It was in 1606, three years before Henry Hudson sailed into American history, on the Half Moon, that the Great Elector of the Palatinate, a true Defender of the "faith once delivered to the saints," laid out Mannheim on a new plan. Most European cities, built on mediæval or feudalistic plans, were crowded and cramped within walls, with crooked streets, undrained, and liable to the recurring pestilence called the plague. In hot weather, the avenues were noisome. It 'was the general custom to let the pigs loose at night, to feed on the garbage thrown from the windows. The new city of Mannheim, besides being well drained, was laid out with thoroughfares at right angles. They were thus open to the sunlight.

Even finer than the form was the spirit of Mannheim. The Elector, champion of freedom of conscience, who invited twenty-five thousand Huguenots to settle in Berlin, gave welcome in his domain to all these fleeing from the clerical oppression of the churchianity that had, in so large a measure, driven out the spirit of Christianity. Frankfort had been the focus of freedom, but now Mannheim excelled. Thousands of Walloon and other oppressed folk thronged to the new city of refuge and found peace and prosperity. After 1685, when Louis XIV revoked the Edict of Nantes, a second great immigration from France met welcome. The city was

then enlarged, and the thrifty and skillful Huguenots who had made fortunes were able to assist their
poorer brethren elsewhere.

As early as 1554, there went out from Mannheim,
the capital city, hundreds of Walloons to a lovely
valley three or four leagues distant, to make a settlement which was fitly named Frankenthal — the Valley of the Free. To the story of this place we now
turn, for over two thirds of the names on the rolls of
the Walloon churches at this place were reproduced
in Nova Belgica, or can be read, in more or less altered form, in our city directories. Some of the families of Walloon descent, in the Empire State still
preserve the letters of dismission from the pastors
and churches of Frankenthal.

One of the most energetic of the Walloon pioneers
in America was Louis du Bois, born in 1627 at Lille,
an old Belgic-French city and destined to make a
name and settlement in the middle region of the
Hudson, between New York and Albany. He led a
colony and founded New Paltz on the Hudson.

From Lille, the Walloon city of weavers and textiles, then situated on Belgic soil, there began, about
1647, a migration eastward of these Bible readers
into the lower Palatinate, on the Rhine, where was
freedom of religion. Their old home land had been
seized by Louis XIV, but for those who suffered, a
change from Spanish to French bigotry was no improvement. Whether their masters were Spanish or
French mattered little, for both were tyrants of the

peculiarly Latin order. So in the "Paltz," as the Walloons called the German State, where also were Waldenses and a few people from the British Isles, they found peace and home. In America their haven of refuge was fitly named New Paltz, or the New Palatinate. Near by was the larger and older settlement of Wiltwick — much later called Kingston and for a time the capital of the State, at whose early history we shall now glance.

In Mannheim, both before and after the Revocation of the Edict of Nantes, many Huguenots found refuge, as has been said. It is even possible that there was not a year, from 1624 to 1700, and certainly there was not a decade, during which the ships floating the flag of the Dutch Republic did not bring Walloon or French Huguenots from Germany to America.

In Mannheim, Louis du Bois married a Walloon maiden, and two sons, Abraham and Isaac, were born to them. Then preferring the American wilderness and the red savages, with the risks of tomahawk and scalping knife, to the Inquisition and galleys under such kings as ruled in his day, he started for the New World, with his fellow believers. After sailing down the Rhine, into the Republic, in the spring-time of 1660, he left for America in the ship Gilded Otter. This early season was chosen so as to have crops and food before winter. Other Walloon families followed this same year.

On setting foot on Manhattan, instead of seeing

the solid stone structures of the Old World — the splendid churches of ancient fame and glory and the ornate town halls in their old home — they beheld about two hundred poorly built houses. These sheltered over fourteen hundred souls. Inside the fort, on Manhattan, were the Dutch church and the Director's house and gardens. As in the northern Netherlands, there was a windmill in one of the bastions and the tricolor flag, orange, white, and blue, waved over all. The hateful monopolies — especially that one of bolted flour, to be done only on Manhattan, so enriching to the city folk, but cursed by every farmer and sure to foment trouble — were not as yet.

The first party of pioneers decided to settle at Esopus. This place, or rather region, central between New York and Albany, had been named by the Indians. By nature it was very lovely, with grand vistas, having the Catskills in their majesty of walls of azure, filling the western background, while the glorious Hudson fronted all. The country was well watered, for the affluents of the mountain-born rain stream drained and gave entrance into a large area and fertile territory rich in game.

Fair indeed is Nature's setting of both Esopus and Wiltwick, or Rondout and Kingston, with sky, water, and land making a picture of unfading beauty. The alluring valley, the lordly river, the picturesque scenery delighted the newcomers. The Walkill, or Walloon's Kill, drains a fertile area in two States and takes its name from the initial settlers. Not far away, a mile or so, was founded the new village, later called Hurley. The names of the settlements around the former capital of the Empire State are well worthy of study. The Dutch name of the colony that became Kingston was given in compliment to the Indian owners. It was called Wiltwick, that is, the town of Good Will, for the red men gave freely the site.

All Nature seemed to smile a welcome. Even the savages had obeyed the mandate of the Great Spirit, to subdue and replenish the earth, so that farm lands, already prepared by human hands, awaited the seed and toil of the newcomers. Nevertheless, desolation was impending. To ascertain why the menace impended, we must look at the first owners of the soil.

History compels us to the conviction that the white man, in the plenitude of his conceit as superior, and his pride in a higher civilization, actually debauched the savage and retarded his steady evolution. Slowly but surely the Indians had been rising in the scale of progress. When Europeans appeared, they for a time checked, instead of developing, his culture. For gain, the white trader sold the red man guns and powder, in exchange for his beaver skins and acres. Yet when the latent fire of excited animal passion was let loose, both life and land, and morals were burned up in the flames of mutual hatred. Soon becoming expert gunmen, the tribes began first to decimate and finally to exter-

minate each other, and to make of themselves
over the whole continent nuisances as pestiferous as
wolves or serpents. Because of this, they invited extermination at the hands of more civilized human beings; so that to-day, only the names of the mountains and the rivers echo in the void, where no Indians are, but whose fathers, by thousands, were
once lords of the soil. In the white man's histories,
we are told that the red man "would not accept our
civilization." Yet we are constrained to ask why
should they — if built on strong drink and murderous weapons?

Taking the next step in their progress downward,
the savages turned their guns against the white
man. Then the old fable of the eagle, wounded to
death by the shaft feathered with its own plumage,
was actualized in blood and fire.

In regions more westerly, issuing not only from
pits and hollows in the ground, or from crevices of
the rocks, but even uprising from flowing streams
and gurgling brooks, were both the mineral oil which
we call petroleum, and the inflammable vapor to
which we give the name of natural gas. Within the
memory of men now living, this gas has been utilized for heat and illumination. Corporations now
harness and sell for coin that of which the aborigines knew not the value, any more than that of
the metallic ores under their feet. It was one of the
amusements of the Indian children to apply fire and
light the bubbles and tiny mists from the marshes.

By the same means, they made the crimson tongues
of flame rise out of, or play on the surface, even, of
the ice-cold, rippling current. This was their game
of "icy-hot," even before the modern invention of
the "thermos bottle" thus advertised. Hence the
name, whether the flame came from swamp or rock
fissure, of "fire water" applied to the white man's
distillations and devilish concoctions.

The solid black mixture of saltpeter, sulphur, and
charcoal and the liquid poison wrought together for
the mutual destruction of red and white man. In both
cases, the ancient truth was verified: "At last it
biteth like a serpent and stingeth like an adder."
Where there was one settler killed because of firearms at the hands of Indians, there were probably a
dozen red men shot to death by murderers of their
own race, in internecine feuds and battles. The efficient causes also of most of the so-called "massa-
cres" of white by red men were gunpowder and rum.
In other cases, Indian vengeance, in return for white
man's brutalities, explained what was too readily
called a "mysterious Providence." In the end, the
weapons, both solid and liquid, together with the
diseases of the palefaces, meant what was well-nigh
extermination of the savages. What the Inquisition
and the tyrant rulers in Europe signified to Bible
readers, compelling exile and movement westward,
the white man's "fire," in both his iron tubes and his
demijohns, meant to the Indians. They were steadily driven towards the setting sun.

THE STORY OF THE WALLOONS

No more blameworthy than other European settlers, from Florida to Maine, the colonists at New
Paltz were soon to suffer, through both cause and effect, from firearms and fire water, and more immediately because of the Indian policy of the honest but
autocratic and irascible Stuyvesant. His methods
were not those of Peter Minuit, Arendt Van Curler,
Roger Williams, or William Penn. To the deviltry
of firearms and fire water Stuyvesant added a crime
which no Indian was known to forgive — that of
slave-driving. Africa, but not America, might carry
such a cross.

The first of the greatest mistakes of this brave old
warrior was typical of his age. In his severity of intolerance in religion, in narrow-mindedness, and in
government, he was an average magistrate of the
century. The second mistake, which involved a dis-
tressing war, and legacies of hate unquenched for
generations, lay in his ignorance of Indian psychology, while underrating the courage of the freeman of
the forest. The negro, belonging to the most patient
of races, might be made a slave, but not the Indian.

After the first Esopus war, Stuyvesant, because a
man of his time and therefore well able to do some
things almost unthinkable to a Netherlands Christian of to-day, sent some of his Indian prisoners as
slaves to Curaçoa, in the West Indies. This proceeding kindled in the red man's breast the fires of re-
venge.

To add insult to injury, the colonists, violating the

fundamental principle of the Dutch charter, had
built the new village on land claimed by the Indians;
while the older settlers, infatuated with love of gain,
sold guns and rum freely to the red men. Again the
world-old truth, that not money, but the lust for it,
or money-love, is a root of all kinds of evil, was
demonstrated. On the 7th of June, the savages in
a concerted attack wiped out the new village of
New Paltz in fire and blood.

At Wiltwick, the onslaught was less successful.
Warned in time, by mounted men spurring in from
the new village, the settlers, led by the brave young
Domine Blum, fought long and hard and the
drunken brutes and crafty savages were driven off.
Besides over a score of Christians killed, fifty or
more white persons were hurried into captivity. The
Indian had learned from his foe, who sold human
flesh in the market, how to make money by ransom.
It was an old European custom. There were ransom
brokers by the thousands. The complements of
slaves for the French, Spanish, and Italian war galleys were recruited at slave auctions.

So the red men held their prisoners and treated
them decently, awaiting their purchase; meanwhile
building a palisade for defense. Three months
passed in captivity. For the Christians in duress,
daily prayer and the singing of Marot's Psalms
proved their best solace. Then Louis du Bois and
Captain Kragier led the rescuing party.

Once again, in threefold demonstration, it was

shown how foolish is injustice and how inferior, in the fine art of living together, as a means of either protection or redress, is force; how idiotic is the lust for money, and how much more effective, for mutual benefit and equal righteousness, and how practically valuable are a knowledge of psychology and the practice of the Golden Rule — the way of Penn, rather than of Stuyvesant, or of Van Curler rather than Kieft.

To the north, living in Schenectady among the Mohawks, this man, whose name, "Corlaer," is now given to governors and kings as the synonym of righteousness and power, was able by his covenant of mutual justice to protect his settlement, which was immune from attack until after his death. Then French priestcraft and bigotry, having poisoned the minds of the savage perverts, prompted the raid and massacre of 1690, which Leisler had tried to forefend.

One happy incident, the result of the pursuit of the Esopus Indians, was the discovery by du Bois of the lovely Walkill valley, so rich in farm land. Into this earthly paradise, at the base of the Shawungunk mountains, "du Bois the Walloon," in 1663, led enterprising settlers to build their homes. In grateful memory of the hospitality of the Great Elector of the Pfalz they named their new home New Paltz.

In 1664, through treacherous conquest, New Netherland was given a name that had little meaning and no relation either to contemporaneous fact or to its past history. The change in the political status of the New Netherlanders, under the governance of the very untrustworthy Duke of York, who was noted for his voluble but slippery promises, did not put an end to the coming of either Belgic Walloons or French Huguenots. This went steadily on, even though the ecclesiastics of the Anglican religious corporation, "established by law," tried to make American history revert to mediæval conceptions, as we shall see. Against this procedure of prelates, to form a State Church, the Dutch and Walloon majority of inhabitants made stout resistance, even to the victorious end. Hence it was that New York in 1777 led all the States in liberality, granting not only toleration, but absolute liberty of religion to all law-abiding citizens. Then the hope and vision of William the Silent, the far-seeing, became fruition and reality; while the very first amendment to the national constitution was against any introduction into the United States of religion "by law established."

CHAPTER XXIII

THE ENGLISH CONQUEST

Two of the worst kings that ever sat on the throne of England were the Stuarts, Charles II and James II. In addition to other lapses from integrity, both aspired to capture New Netherland, in a time of peace. After hoodwinking the Dutch ambassador, Charles II sent an armed squadron, by which conquest was made and possession taken. The flag of a monarchy, instead of a republic, waved over Manhattan in 1664.

Yet if one seeks to record facts with the honesty of the contemporary writer, Bishop Burnet, the reader may well ask, "Was this treacherous business a success? Was the conquest nominal or real? Did New York become a little England, or more sturdily American?"

The real history of New York, from 1664 to 1775, is one of social and religious, even more than political opposition to what English statesmen and governors tried, with more or less purity of motives, to introduce into what had been a province of the Dutch Republic. The pith of the story of New Netherland is found in the popular struggles against the tyranny of a grasping corporation, the covetousness of patroons, and the folly of men ever looking towards selfish ends. The desire of the people was for

THE ENGLISH CONQUEST

the same freedom which had been enjoyed at home. Wearied by the long conflict, they hoped for even more liberty under English rule. In this they were disappointed. It was not until after twenty years of English rule that they arrived at the same point left off under the Dutch — the election of a popular representative assembly, which they had gained in 1663.

For from the very first, the English lords of Church and State made the usual blunders of most conquerors in failing to understand the psychology of the nominally conquered. The initial purpose, ever persevered in by the autocratic king, the lords temporal and spiritual, and the commercially-minded Commons in Parliament, seemed to be to inflict on the colonists the features which they had most hated, and of which they had left Europe to be forever rid. These were autocracy, Church and State in political combination, the surviving forms of feudalism and privilege, the arrant nonsense of "divine right," and an aristocracy based on birth. These were what, for their weal or woe, the colonists detested and were determined to do away with. In a word, they wanted and resolved to have only what in Europe was good, and that which they deemed just to themselves as men and fair to humanity. What had bred persecution, cruelty, and bloodshed, they were a unit in their purpose to leave and keep behind.

The influence of the new environment had already

begun to affect them. Amid the freedom of the virgin forests, with vistas of boundless expansion, they were determined to get what they wanted, even if in their methods of seeking it they were no gentler than their oppressors, to whom the rack, the scourge, the gallows, the axe, and the sword had been familiar methods of persuasion. These people did not jest at scars, for the reason that they had felt wounds.

Yet it would be absurd to apply "the frontier theory" to explain fully why the people of New York — the Americans, such as they were or are, either then or now — differ so notably from Englishmen. Already even in 1664, the new type of man was forming. So much French, Dutch, and other strains of blood, in a people and in a country in which seventeen languages were spoken, made it impossible for the insular institutions of England to work in harmony with those on Manhattan and the neighboring islands, or in the valleys of our broad rivers.

Undoubtedly these royal agents in power, with old-world notions, meant well. Some were less grasping and covetous than others, nor were they hidebound creatures of tradition and routine. Several of the king's appointees were men of conscience and integrity; but in the main, the less the doings of the English governors from 1664 to 1776 are exposed to view, the more we, of English descent, at least, and proud of our birthright and inheritance, think of the dear Fatherland whence our Welsh, English, Scotch, and Irish ancestors came.

THE ENGLISH CONQUEST

In the last analysis, we may say that in growth toward nationality the "Continental" prevailed over purely traditional elements and the local spirit. The idea of a union of all the colonies, first suggested by Leisler, gained a strength that steadily increased, through the logic of the events of July 4, 1776, of June 14, 1777, and of September 17, 1787. In succession, the Declaration of Independence, the flag of the Stars and Stripes, and the Constitution formed by "the people of the United States" took their place in the annals of mankind and "a more perfect union" was formed.

The ideas generated on American soil came into collision with those which honest and capable British statesmen felt were sound and even altruistic. Americans, following the democratic principles of the Netherlands Communes and the motto of 1477, "No taxation without consent," demanded representation in Parliament and raised the cry, "No taxation without representation." Even the American opposition to bad British government, when better organized in all the colonies, followed closely in its methods those which in Parliament resulted in a better Britain, and in which we on this side of the water rejoice. The outcome in the American Commonwealth redounds to the glory of English history and is part of it.

To this day, also, British folk usually refer to the American Commonwealth as "the States," while good Americans lay emphasis on the *United* States and think of their country in the singular, making use only as a sub-title of the plural. To them, the body is more than its members. It does not contribute to a better understanding between Englishmen and Americans to represent the latter as a mere off-shoot of the English stock. It is this unwarranted assumption of wholly English culture and preponderating English blood, that has more than once embittered international relations. Even such historians as Edward A. Freeman, Goldwin Smith, and James Bryce have proceeded on this misleading theory, and many publicists and societies, and the English press, still refuse to face the facts, which were as patent in the seventeenth as in the twentieth century. In their research into documents, governmental acts, and things purely external, scholars have forgotten to study the man, the real American, in whose veins flow such generous streams of French, Dutch, Irish, Scotch, Welsh, German, and Scandinavian blood. No critical scholar can to-day accept the old notion, almost crystallized in a sacred tradition, that before the Revolution "ninety-eight per cent of New Englanders were of English descent."

From the very first, ecclesiastics and economists began to attempt the making of the American colonies, that were already cosmopolitan in texture and spirit, a second England, instead of even a second United Kingdom — wherein were the unconquerable Scots, who kept their church and law forms; the valiant Welsh, who never gave up their inherited culture; and the Irish, both of Ulster and the South, among whom Norman feudalism never took root. In America, these belated Norman ideas would not work any more, but vastly less, than in Ireland, Scotland, and Wales.

The absurdity of trying to establish the Anglican machinery of religion, when relatively there were only a few hundred English people, or conformists, in the colony of New York, was attempted and obstinately persevered in, only to meet with hatred, defiance, and defeat. The overwhelming majority of Free Churchmen were desperately determined not to wear the Anglican fetters. The spirit of the Beggars, of the men of the Half Moon, of the Walloons and the Huguenots, of the Waldenses, of the Swiss — who had humbled Charles the Bold — when challenged and affronted, kept rising. Those who counted all gain but loss, in order to keep conscience free, were unitedly against the schemes of absentee landlords and of over-sea prelates bound to a throne, and these protesting elements were as a unit in their resistance.

On the economic side, the people of the hinterland were infuriated at the English monopolies, which were centralized on lower Manhattan. When British manufacturers, using the power of Parliament and the Crown, first ruined the Irish manufacturers and then attempted to smother the infant industries of the colonists, the effect was to breed a spirit of sullen determination and invincible resistance. This false theory led to emigration from North Ireland to America, on a large scale, giving our fathers a tremendous reinforcement, especially on the frontiers.

When, further, the English governor, among people who from the invention of printing and long before Milton's voice was heeded in England had gloried in a free press, attempted to muzzle the German Zenger's newspaper, the Scotchman, Andrew Hamilton, championed freedom of speech and of the press. By his learning, acuteness, and eloquence he made appeal to law that was older than crowns or thrones.

Zenger was acquitted and the Dutch idea of the freedom of the press was fixed and later secured in the national constitution. The first amendment to this fundamental law reads: "Congress shall make no law respecting an establishment of religion, or prohibiting the free exercise thereof, or abridging the freedom of speech or of the press, or the right of the people peaceably to assemble and to petition the government for a redress of grievances."

Without a knowledge of the interior life and working of the Reformed Dutch Church, with which most of the Walloons and French Huguenots and many other immigrants coalesced, whose constitution seems a miniature of that of the United States of 1787, it is next to impossible to understand the inner history of the colony named successively Nova Belgica, New Netherland, and New York. This is true as simple matter of fact, for the people of the great city and State ultimately divided themselves socially less by race, politics, or economic interests, than by church affiliations, into Dutch, French, and English. He cannot be at home in the story, either of the Empire State or of Pennsylvania, who is not intimately acquainted with these phenomena.

The struggle against the English governors and prelates from 1664 to 1705, and the partial success of episcopacy, resulted in what, by the English party in the colony, was wholly undesired and unexpected; viz., the obtaining of charters for their churches by the Dutch — which no others, outside of the Episcopal establishment, were able to secure — with later the establishment of Rutgers College at New Brunswick, New Jersey, and Union College at Schenectady, New York.

Such a view of the facts helps to explain not only a half-century of Leislerism, but also the craving for that union of all the colonies, which originated in the Middle Region, of which Jacob Leisler was the champion whose example Benjamin Franklin did but follow.

After the Articles of Confederation, which were much like those of the old Dutch Republic, there issued the Constitution of 1787. This, with its system of checks and balances in government, seems nigh to perfection; yet every one of its federal precedents is borrowed, with vast improvements, from those of the United States of the Netherlands. Franklin, Madison, Hamilton, and Jefferson, even in their criticisms and rejection, in 1787, of the outworn

Dutch system, confess great obligations, theirs and ours. Apart from numerous passages in their own writings, one has but to read "The Federalist" to see this. There was no blind copying, but selection.

When, to cite one of many similar examples, the English Governor Fletcher, in March, 1693, in an angry speech to the members of Assembly, which consisted mostly of Dutch and Walloon members, said, "There are none of you but what are big with the privileges of Englishmen and Magna Charta," he meant, even as his acts showed, that it was upon those principles of feudalism, which are embodied in that noble document, rather than upon its provisions for the freedom and protection of villeins, commoners, or the people, that he laid his personal emphasis. The Netherlanders, speakers of both French and Dutch, as well as the Scotch and Germans, were unable then, even as intelligent Americans are now, to see the real facts in the same light as this English interpreter of Magna Charta. Fletcher's notions were wholly of the conventional order, such as those with which after-dinner orators even yet often regale, while deluding, their hearers.

Fletcher at once proceeded to establish a State Church. This enterprise was exceedingly distasteful, if not insulting, to the overwhelming majority of the non-English British folk, Walloons and others; while by the Dutch, especially, who were equally proud, with the Anglicans, of belonging to a national church, the innovation was directly and stoutly resisted. So this relic of Latin centralization and Norman feudalism was fastened only upon certain parishes, in four only, out of the ten counties of New York.

Furthermore, what seemed positively ridiculous, in the eyes of the majority of the people, was the attempt of Governor Fletcher and his successors to inflict upon them and create on American soil what they were thankful, every day of their lives, they had not: viz., a "House of Lords, Spiritual and Temporal" in the scheme of "King, Lords, and Commons." Even the idea of "Commons" was distasteful, not only to the non-English, but to the Puritans. These, in the army of the Commonwealth, had changed the official vocabulary from "common soldiers" to "privates" — the term now universal.

When the people demanded a popular assembly, to make the laws and vote the taxes, Governor Fletcher, in his wrath at such a demand, uttered words that roused still more anger. Those who were at first sullen became defiant. Said he:

"You ought to remember that you have but a third share in the legislative power of the government.... You ought to let the Council have a share. They are in the nature of a House of Lords, or Upper House."

All this was exactly what the men of New York were determined not to remember, but to forget.

Again, by aping the ways of other unwitting colonizers of America, Fletcher and his still more foolish

successor, Cornbury, unknowingly became promo-
ters of the further colonization of New Jersey and
helped to build up Pennsylvania and Delaware. The
number of Dutch and Walloon churches doubled
during the first generation of English rule. When
Fletcher's little finger of oppression became Cornbury's right hand of autocracy, and the English
whips had become scorpions, the results were large
migrations into the adjoining Quaker colony, where
was mild republican government.

New Jersey, instead of scanty settlements of
the pioneers, sailors, stevedores, and longshoremen,
chiefly ex-servants of the West India Company, now
grew in population faster than New York. There
went out into the Raritan valley, in a total of many
thousands, in bands, caravans, and whole churches,
communities of Walloon and Dutch both, the descendants of these lovers of freedom who wanted
better government. By these refined and cultivated
people, friends of religion and education, schools and
colleges were reared as bulwarks against both "the
puny skeptic's hand" and "the bigot's blinded
rule." They made the wilderness blossom. New
Jersey became a garden state.

These people, thus "outed and expelled," thrived
on oppression. Instead of there being in 1664 four or
five Dutch churches — the vital units of their organization — in which also were most of the Walloons,
with services and sermons in French, there were,
in the year 1700, twenty-nine Reformed churches.

THE ENGLISH CONQUEST

These were under the care of the Classis of Amsterdam, and a majority of them, with a noble history, exist to-day. In time the Walloon and Huguenot congregations on Long, Staten, and Manhattan Islands, at New Paltz and in the Hudson, Mohawk, and Raritan valleys, which had cordially fraternized with the Dutch, ultimately coalesced with them. Still later, a large number, more especially of Huguenots, coming in directly from France or from the West Indies, became Episcopal and adopted the Prayer Book and Anglican ritual. Æsop's parable of the storm and the sunshine, the traveler and his cloak, was again illustrated. It was the intimate knowledge of economic conditions in the West Indies that enabled so many Huguenots, in both the colonies and the States, to become wealthy merchants, such as Faneuil, Gerard, Hilligas, and scores of others.

During the Revolution, no body of Christians excelled those in the Reformed churches in furnishing soldiers to the Continental armies; nor, in proportion to their numbers, more patriotic chaplains and ministers — with a British price set on their heads. To scan the lists of the official records of militia and regular troops bearing French, Dutch, German, Swiss, Scotch, Welsh, and Irish names, is an inspiration. The roster foreshadowed Distinctive America, and the fusing of all minor elements into one nobler mould for a State supreme, with a spirit of tolerance and compromise that was to react first upon the colonies and then upon the nation at large.

THE STORY OF THE WALLOONS

The idea of "the people" as a constituent part, or officially recognized entity, was not unknown in America outside of New England. In reality, the first occurrence, in any American legal document, of the phrase, "the people," was in the Charter of Liberties granted by the Duke of York to his new colony, amid the rejoicings of the Manhattanese and the interior folks. The man who was to become James II of England affixed his signature September 17, 1683, to the Charter of Liberties, and commented favorably upon it. He even promised further privileges. The text of this state paper reads:

"The supreme legislative authority under His Majesty and His Royal Highness, James, Duke of York, Albany, etc., Lord Proprietor of said province, shall forever reside in the governor, council, and *the people* met in general assembly."

Yet what Stuart sovereign ever kept a promise, or cared for truth? On February 6, 1665, the Duke became a king. The Charter was first kept in London, and then, by secret instructions to Governor Dongan, dated May 29, 1686, "repealed and disallowed." This Irish Catholic Christian gentleman, noble statesman, and wise governor, who had made "the people" so happy by telling them of the gracious favor of his master, was left in the lurch, to explain a royal perjuror's acts as best he could.

Yet there are those who wonder at Leisler's "usurpation" and the tremendous popular feeling, Dutch and Huguenot, that was behind him, persisting through generations. The staunch loyalty, during the Revolution, to the Continental Congress, of the pastors of these churches, in which the people elected their own officers, and in which the spirit of democracy was unquenchable, surprised the London statesmen, who threw on others the odium of failure in the "Scotch War."

On the purely social side of the question, whether the "English conquest" was nominal or real, or New York was ever, in any but a very nebulous sense of the term, an English colony, one has but to read a book full of inside, non-official, but none the less real history, like "The Goede Vrouw of Mana-ha-ta," by Mrs. John Van Rensselaer, to realize what little impress English insular notions, methods, and manners made upon the cosmopolitan people of New York. "The History of the City of New York in the Seventeenth Century," by Mrs. Schuyler Van Rensselaer, gives in accurate and judicial form a clear picture of the noble addition made to the American composite by the better sort of English people, who came, not in overweening pride, "to tarry for a night," or until sufficient pounds, shillings, and pence had been scooped into their coffers, but who, with gifts, graces, character, and sterling virtues, enriched the Empire commonwealth.

CHAPTER XXIV
WHO WAS JACOB LEISLER?

Was Jacob Leisler à German? I, for one, believe he was a Walloon. This successful merchant, far-seeing statesman, who first proposed a union of all the colonies — eminent Christian, church officer, champion of the people, unsleeping foe of monopoly, victim of a drunken governor and his parasites but justified by Parliament and vindicated by posterity and history — has been called by the prejudiced and ignorant, a "usurper" and a "low-lived German." Can we, amid the fog and storm of hate on the one side, and excess of adulation on the other, distinguish the true lineaments? Perhaps we may better ask, "Has not the storm cleared?"

Frankfort, in Protestant Germany, was a notable rendezvous for the refugees, seeking "freedom to worship God," whether from the Marian persecutions in England, or from despotic France and the Spanish Netherlands. In Germany these exiles took German names from choice, by adoption, or by translation or transliteration of their own, and became as German as the natives. Among others was a minister of the gospel, supposed, without any proof, by later writers to be "a German." In all probability, according to the general and persistent belief among those who knew them best, the Leislers,

STATUE OF JACOB LEISLER
At New Rochelle, N. Y.

father and son, were of the Huguenot faith and from the Belgic Netherlands, or France. The ruins of the old French Reformed or Huguenot Church in Frankfort may still be seen between the Catholic and Protestant church edifices of to-day. There is also a "Walloon Strasse," or street.

How Jacob's early life was spent we do not know. Like so many young men of adventurous spirit, in the days when the soldier of fortune was a social product, his trade reckoned honorable and his figure a prominent one in many countries, and when America was the Land of Promise, Jacob, going to Holland, enlisted in the service of the West India Company. He took passage in the ship Otter, sailing April 24, 1660, for New Netherland. In the list of soldiers, his name is written "Jacob Leysseler of Francfort," but his clearly read autograph appears as "Jacob Leisler." When on Manhattan, he found himself indebted to the Company for passage and extras to the extent of nearly one hundred florins. So, like tens of thousands of other settlers in the Middle Colonies and even in New England, beginning with the Pilgrims, he was an "engagé," or "redemptioner."

Yet he lived to become a man of wealth and station. He was most probably "illiterate" only in English, which was then spoken by a small number of people in New York. Unfortunately for religion, the ministers — who, alas, are usually too apt to favor the pew-renting, salary-paying, well-to-do part of society — were, in the main, against Leisler. One

237

of the Dutch Domines he called a "cockeran." This showed that Leisler the layman was not versed in the minutiæ of those incessant controversies that curse the church. In the Republic, Vœtius and Cocceius, or Voet and Koch, were at that time in the cock-pit. Those who have looked on their portraits at Leyden University and read Dutch ecclesiastical history, or one of the few good books in English on "The Reformed Church in the Netherlands" — for example, Maurice G. Hansen's sketch, which is the best of any of the kind on this subject — will see how the virus of controversy penetrated even to the women, and was exhibited particularly at the parlor windows on Sunday afternoons. One, Voet, represented the mediæval schoolmen and ultra-orthodoxy. Koch, the liberal, introduced the newer school of biblical criticism, and held non-Hebrew and non-Puritan ideas about the Sabbath, which were considered "loose" by opponents. In a word, here was a phase of controversy as old as Cain and Abel, and as new as the present year, and which will never cease while knowledge so rapidly grows and human nature is so slow to improve.

All these controversies affected thousands of the Walloons in the Dutch Republic. It was largely through their mediating spirit, influence, and writings, that reconciliation and peace were brought about after "the second eighty years' war."

These excitements in Patria, the Fatherland, stirred mightily the Walloons and Dutch in New

WHO WAS JACOB LEISLER?

York. The controversy shook the Reformed, of both races and languages, from the peach orchards below Cape Henlopen to the broom-corn fields of the Mohawk flats. The records of the synods, which were held before the final settlement, at Schenectady, of Reverend Petrus Tassemacher, who was a Cocceian, while the other four Dutch Domines were Vœtians, show this. In the case of the young Domine on the Mohawk, his story was soon told. The minions of Louis XIV and "the King's religion" in Canada stirred up the red savages to burn the frontier village and slaughter the inhabitants. He was first killed and his body was thrown into the blazing furnace of his former home.

Leisler was of the old school of orthodoxy, a Vœtian, and he behaved like other church folks; but not being versed in scholastic theology, is said to have called one of his pulpit opponents a "cockeran" minister, when perhaps he meant to say "Cocceian." Yet if he used the Dutch, instead of the latinized form of Koch's name, his was not much of a solecism. Moreover, it is likely that the caricatures, lampoons, and controversial woodcuts for which the Dutch were so famous had reached America. The Dutch funny fellows who in 1619 chased hens in Leyden shouting "arme haenen" (poor hens) for Arminians were quite capable of a "comic supplement" fully equal to those in our American age of Sunday newspapers.

Of course such a proof of "illiteracy" was conclusive. It is more than probable that the Domines denounced Leisler, more on account of his lack of scholastic inerrancy than because of his politics. It is even quite possible that the supposed solecism, "cockeran," came first from the lips of a tale-bearer, and not out of Leisler's mouth.

The probabilities and deductions, from the available data in records and testimonies, favor the idea that Jacob Leisler was by birth and inheritance a Walloon. It was the popular belief at the time. In his Introduction to the "History of New Rochelle," by Jeanne A. Forbes, Mr. Caryl Coleman, embodying the contemporaneous view in Leisler's lifetime, has written of him thus: "A well-to-do and rich merchant, a man of French ancestry, but born in Germany . . . a pronounced anti-Jacobin, with strong democratic tendencies."

Neither a polished courtier, nor a Christian who considered a knowledge of scholastic philosophy necessary to faith or salvation, nor a fanatic, nor a fool, nor a usurper, Leisler was the man needed for the hour. It was no disgrace that a man of travel and experience, able to speak two languages, and who had had experiences among the Turks, should be deemed "illiterate" by persons who knew only one form of speech. To him, the overworked symbol of the cross, as to Endicott of Salem, was as hateful as the green flag of Islam, or the red crescent standard of the Ottomans.

The life in America of Jacob Leisler is well known.

WHO WAS JACOB LEISLER?

The next year, 1661, after his arrival, when Stuyvesant discharged sixscore soldiers, most of whom returned to Europe, Leisler remained in the service.
From the first, he was a man of decided religious
views and character, with an intense bitterness
against those political churches which in God's name
had ravaged the Palatinate, driven him from home,
and put to death men who differed in opinion. Entering commercial life, he prospered greatly and married into one of the families that considered themselves "the quality." Active and zealous in the
Church, he was chosen an officer, becoming first a
deacon and then an elder in the Consistory. In
every way he was a popular or "people's man." In
insight, sympathies, understanding, and average
abilities, he represented three fourths of the people.
He despised the so-called "aristocracy," whether in
or out of the Church, and of both the real and the
sham order. Unfortunately, of the latter sort there
were not a few in that minority, of British folk and
some others, that basked in the favor of the English
governor and his petty court. In giving expression
to his feelings, Leisler was sometimes rather noisy
and ostentatious. He imitated too closely his English predecessors. Nor was he a shining example of
that tact and courtesy which we associate with Huguenots. In a word, under the menace of French
conquest he repaid his enemies and those he considered such in their own coin.

  None, more than Leisler, knew the danger from

France, from Canada, and from the forces which, outwardly, in sheep's clothing wore religion as if for the salvation of souls, while inwardly ravening wolves. None of his predecessors, Dutch or English, had put or kept in order the defenses of New York City, or of the frontiers, with an energy equal to his. To this the "Battery," in its name, still bears witness. None more vigorously than Leisler dared to attack and break up the detestable monopolies governed from the south end of Broadway. He promised, in writing, the Schenectady farmers, that he would seek redress for them. When his letters were found, by the French marauders and their savage allies, on the streets of that village, they were soaked in the blood of those who cherished them as tokens of economic salvation.

The possibility, at which his detractors sneered, became, on February 9, 1690, a reality, written in blood and fire. No one discerned so clearly the need of colonial unity and the impending dangers from a raid from Canada, of savages whose lust for blood was heated by bigotry and religious hate instilled in them by white men from France. On all his fears and warning, the massacre at Schenectady — Albany being saved only because the intense cold diverted attack — was a commentary in red.

Perhaps Leisler was fanatical in his religious beliefs and hatred of the kind of Frenchmen of 1690 and the France of Louis XIV. He was an intense and fiery anti-Jacobin also. But why? Not because

WHO WAS JACOB LEISLER?

he was a "German," as Bancroft and most of the encyclopædias and their copyists say he was, for it is most probable that he was not. Besides Dutch, German, and a little English, his speech was French. But then, he knew well what most discerning men saw also, that for the French to conquer would be to turn America into the kind of France that then existed. Under that despotism of priestcraft, people were hunted down like wild beasts, and then tortured or killed, or chained to the galley's oar, because they had a conscience and worshiped God in a different way from a colossal egotist, who then called himself "The State," and from his fellow murderers. Had Louis XIV succeeded in capturing New York, the poor Huguenot women would have been made slaves and the men sent to the galleys to spend their lives in exile and drudgery. The literature of men who had toiled in the galleys, including John Knox, and who wrote out their experiences, help us to know how the Huguenots of 1690 felt.

Leisler was determined to defend the New Yorkers against both the English traitor-king, James II, and the gilded tyránt, Louis XIV. He had the people behind him and they looked to him as their protector. If we range the ministers of the Dutch Reformed Church against him, as history records and compels us to do, it is because in their pride of education and love of learning they opposed Leisler more because he was "illiterate," than on account of his politics. Moreover, rough as Leisler was in handling his enemies, he never, like them towards him, thirsted for blood.

In fact, to sift the whole matter, the opposition to Leisler was almost entirely personal. The "quality" felt that one of their number ought to have Leisler's place, even as they envied his influence with the overwhelming majority of the people.

What was there, on the other side, to oppose him, and what were the vengeful forces that finally, against all law and decency, had him put to death? Of this legal murder the English Parliament afterward disapproved, reversed the attainder, and vindicated Leisler, doing him just honor. We repeat that whatever Leisler's faults, he had none of the bloodthirstiness of his enemies, who, by pressure brought upon the English governor when in his cups, secured his death. The precedents of 1676 and 1682, in Virginia, of the royal governor's not waiting for the king's order, when thirty-seven men were put to death by this English officer, was followed in Manhattan in 1690.

Neither martyr nor villain, nor a "usurper," Leisler both in his life and in his death wrought a great work for American freedom, law, and order. For thirty years after his death, both parties, named for or against him, rendered it harder and ever more difficult for English governors to try to make of New York a land of belated feudalism, or a new England of the kind that was increasingly obsolescent in the old Mother Land. Leisler's life and death worked for the constant ascendency, in the social and political world, of the once despised lower classes — who needed only education and pure religion to rise higher in the scale.

From one point of view, the history of the United States shames England; from another, it is England's glory. Leisler wrought for the best British elements, which we Americans love and emulate, and against the worst, which we hate and will not have. Furthermore, what was of benefit to New York reacted on all the colonies, even as the spirit and temper of the four Middle States, built on the old Nova Belgica and New Netherland, affected for good the nation, when in 1726 it became independent. There was no colony that surpassed New York in the power of public opinion, nor any that in the initial constitution as a State excelled her in guaranteeing absolute freedom of religion to all.

On the scaffold, forgiving his murderers, Jacob Leisler proved himself a Christian beyond "name, or form, or ritual word," and

> "Like Him with pardon on his tongue
> In midst of mortal pain,
> He prayed for them that did the wrong."

For two centuries the name of Leisler has been the target of malignant abuse and misrepresentation. Yet in our day, Leisler's memory has been cleared by some of the descendants of the very men who had him hanged. The late Dr. A. G. Vermilye, of Wal-

THE STORY OF THE WALLOONS

loon and Huguenot ancestry, by his discussion of
the episode, made useless all previous controversy.
Leisler's statue in bronze at New Rochelle adorns
the place of which he made a peaceful haven for the
victims of French fury.

CHAPTER XXV
WALLOONS BECOME FRENCHMEN

IT may puzzle the average person whose historical reading is defective, to discriminate between "Walloon" and "Huguenot," as these terms are commonly used. The distinction is akin to that between Pilgrim and Puritan, and in phases of religion they are without a real difference. In both cases these speakers of the French and of the English language, respectively, and in all four instances, held to the one faith. The needless confusion is like that of the alleged "conflict" between "science" and "religion" — which is one purely of human limitations and interpretations of the same concept which includes both. It is as near the truth as to talk about the "warfare" between "chemistry" and "science."

Because some Belgic Walloons, already Huguenots, became, under the dictates of autocracy and diplomacy, subjects of the France of Louis XIV, there has been generated more confusion — as if the boundaries of countries in Europe were changeless. After the struggle of arms, directed by Louis XIV, this royal specimen of conceit incarnate, it was decreed by the Treaty of Utrecht, in 1713, that one of the finest and richest areas in "the Spanish Netherlands," or Belgic Land, was to be annexed to France

and to become later the Département du Nord —
the third richest and most populous of the French
administrative units.

Hence the puzzle of the average man, more or less
familiar with the colonial history of New York, to
find on the map of France those cities of Avesnes,
Arras, Valenciennes, Douai, Malplaquet, Lille, with
many towns and villages, which were so long associated with both "Belgian" history and the founding
of New Netherland. Yet the Huguenot Walloons,
whether Netherlanders or Frenchmen, Spanish or
Gallic subjects, were the same in blood and faith and
sterling character.

Hence also the references in documents to
"French" churches in the Dutch Republic, in the
British Isles, and in the German Palatinate; whose
formation was in the sixteenth, not the seventeenth
century, and whose members were almost wholly
Walloons, or Belgians! There are thousands of
Americans, versed in popular but uncritical notions
of genealogy, who imagine they are descended from
Gallic instead of Walloon ancestors.

In a word, hundreds of thousands of people
of Belgic stock and speaking French were made
Frenchmen. In this transfer, willy nilly, of the allegiance of wealthy and industrious people, the
French royal autocrat excelled the Spaniard, or the
Turk, in the deviltry of his oppression and persecution. The aim and purpose of the Grand Monarch,
urged on even more by his colossal vanity than by

THE WALLOON CHURCH IN AMSTERDAM

rancor of religion, so-called, was to become the un-questioned master of the souls as well as the bodies of men.

In this aim, he was baffled by thousands of the brave, who refused to sell their consciences, or their birthright of faith. Those not chained to the oar, or coerced into nominal conformity, sought to escape. In disguise, in peat boats, or in carts under hay or grain, in ships' holds, or on springless wagons through the darkness, on rafts, or by swimming rivers, they took the risk. Aided by friendly brutes or men, they fled by thousands.

Not a few, even when wounded by bullet shots or sword blows, or tracked by bloodhounds, passed the frontiers. The "underground railroad" was no new thing when in the nineteenth century it was dug or built for the black slave escaping from the cotton fields or indigo swamps, in America.

On American soil in an earlier epoch, however, the road to freedom was not towards the North Star, but in the direction of the Southern Cross — from New France or Canada into New York and New England.

Comparatively few were the flights made directly from France to America, the land of freedom. In overwhelming majority the refugees made haven by way of the Rhine, the Dutch Republic, Great Britain, or the Caribbean Isles. Then the Huguenots, whether Belgian Walloon or Protestant French, flowed together in one stream. Hence, after A.D.

1713, the distinctive story of the fugitive Walloons as Belgic folk comes to an end.

In the same manner and for the same reason, the Pilgrim story after 1690 loses distinction from that of the Puritan — both to be virtually forgotten for nearly two centuries, but to rise to the resurrection of recognition and glory after 1750. By that time, the old homes of Bradford, Brewster, and Robinson at Scrooby and Austerfield had been discovered with the aid of the Yorkshire historian, Reverend John Hunter. In the researches of the Dutch pastors Kist and Scheffer among the documents in Dutch archives, the story of the English Separatists stood forth plain and detailed.

The tens of thousands of her best people whom France exiled in the name of God found homes in Germany, Sweden, Switzerland, Denmark, the British Isles, and in South Africa. More numerously than elsewhere, they fled into the Dutch Republic, thence across the Atlantic to Massachusetts and Connecticut, New York, Pennsylvania, New Jersey, Virginia, and South Carolina. They brought, for the making of the American Commonwealth, the greatest wealth that to any country is conceivable — the riches of good and intelligent men and women of character, industry, and culture.

In Germany to the number of thirty thousand or more they enriched the realm with new trades and industries, and soon made the region desolated by the armies of Louis XIV blossom again. In Berlin,

WALLOONS BECOME FRENCHMEN

given at first the royal stables to live in, these Huguenots, of 1672 and later, came to dwell in palaces and became more Prussian than the Prussians themselves. Yet they kept up preaching and worship in French, even to their quarter-millennial celebration in July, 1922.

Even yet many Europeans wonder why it is that the United States of America is so rich in money and brains, with free religion and self-government; but history makes it plain.

While these Huguenot refugees were from every part of France, the majority came from Normandy and what is now the Département du Nord, much of it being formerly Belgic Land, so that of the whole number of Huguenot refugees in America, from 1600 to 1700, the Walloons probably formed at least one third, and possibly one half.

One may ask, "How did so many Huguenots, who were very poor, secure passage across the Atlantic?" The answer is, in the same manner as the poverty-stricken Pilgrim Fathers of Massachusetts who were "redemptioners," like the poor Walloons, to the several colonies, or like the Germans in Pennsylvania; that is, they paid later by their toil, when in America, for land-transit in Europe and for their sea-outfit and ocean passage, with years of work for those who had sent them out. Their services were mortgaged. They "redeemed" or bought themselves back by paying or working out their debt to their masters — whom we of to-day should call capitalists. Yet many of the refugees from the West Indies were persons of wealth, and possibly a majority of American fortunes, before 1800, made in commerce, were amassed by the Huguenot merchants.

The French, in sending colonies to the "West Indies," especially to the island of St. Christopher, or St. Kitts, were among the first to practice the custom of "redemptioning." They called the passengers under bond "engagés," because their labor for a term of years was previously mortgaged, or engaged, by the ship owners or trading and transportation companies. Most of the ancestors of the best people in the United States were "redemptioners," even when not called by that name.

Long before the Revocation of the Edict of Nantes, in 1685, the Huguenots had been shut out from Canada by the royal edicts, so that even on this part of American soil they were hunted down and deported as if they were vermin. Between the years 1657 and 1663, especially, thousands of these people came from Canada into the Dutch and English American colonies.

CHAPTER XXVI

GREATER WALLOONIA

NEITHER a description of Belgic Land nor an outline of its history would be complete, without mention of a certain piece of territory beyond the western frontier of Belgium.

What is now the Département du Nord in France, which, next to that of the Seine, is the richest and most populous, was once a part of the Walloon's home land.

The larger part of this French territory, with its rich cities, its prosperous manufactures, and its affluent agriculture, is inhabited by people whose ancestors were Belgic. In the processes, first of coveting and then of seizing land, the European sovereigns have ever been past masters. It was after many tortuous mazes of diplomacy that this region, following the Treaty of Aix-la-Chapelle — itself a Walloon city — became part of France.

Louis XIV was the autocrat of all France and her possessions in various parts of the world. In 1690, to please him and his mistress, Madame de Maintenon, the French of Canada, with their savage allies, hoped to drive the English and Dutch out of New York and possess it for France. Inflamed with fanaticism and lust for the scalps of women and children, they set forth on snowshoes in midwinter, through

the deep drifts and over the long space between the
St. Lawrence and the Mohawk rivers, hoping to capture Albany. Owing to the intense cold, they were
able only to destroy the little village of Schenectady
and then retreat, pursued by the colonial militia and
the friendly Mohawks. Between hardships, hunger,
and attack, only a remnant of the raiders reached
Canada. This was all that came of the plan con-
cocted in Paris to conquer all New York. So the
energies of the French in America, led by d'Iberville,
were directed to the settlement of Louisiana.

Meanwhile, in the southern part of the province,
the Huguenot refugees from their home land and the
places of their dispersion in Germany were pouring
into New York.

On the Western Atlantic front, five great sea-
gates swung open wide their portals to admit and
welcome so rich an accession to the American composite. These were at Boston, New York, Philadelphia, Jamestown, and Charleston. Yet of all these
premier seaports, the highest honors of entrance,
welcome and hospitality, belong to the thrice-
named city on Manhattan and to the thrice-named
river, on the bosom of which the incoming ships were
borne. Here their best friend, Jacob Leisler, who
had already personally assisted Huguenots with
money and sympathy, met them with land purchased in their behalf and ready to be occupied by
homes.

As New Paltz in origin, character, and history was

the most distinctively Walloon settlement within the boundaries of the Empire State, so was New Rochelle most notably that of the French Huguenots. With stirring memories of the old city beyond the sea, so long the stronghold of brave defenders against intolerance and bad statesmanship, New Rochelle has been celebrated as one of the noblest types of American municipalities, wherein many creeds and nations dwell in brotherhood.

Was it any wonder that, when safe in America, the Huguenots debated whether their new city of refuge should receive the name of New Rupella or New Rochelle? They would go beyond the memories of war and sieges and famine, to the Rock of Peace in earlier days.

It was in 1628 that the French city fell. Then the remnant, that had survived disease, starvation, and battle, scattered. Under the same "necessity, the tyrant's plea," for national unity — as already made use of in England to drive out to exile the Pilgrims — France cast out her children, to enrich Germany and the United States of America.

Nevertheless, amid all variations of war and peace, fortune and decay, with annoyances as numerous as incredible, during the whole of the seventeenth century, La Rochelle, with the Aunis region, France's smallest province, besides being until the Revocation of 1685 the center of Huguenot life and activity, is the ancestral home of tens of thousands of Americans. Of the fifteen thousand Huguenots who entered Pennsylvania, of the ten thousand in Virginia, and of a number equaling those who settled in the Carolinas and a possibly equal total in New York and New England — quite probably fifty thousand in all before 1750 — the majority could trace their descent to the towns and villages of western France. A large proportion of the remainder were from that northeastern part of the French realm which once was Walloon Land.

Amid the annoyances and the disabilities forced on them, and the obstacles placed on their crossing the French frontiers, those who were left behind and who would not sell their consciences lived on and even formed "The Church in the Desert." As secretly as the first Christians in the Roman catacombs, but as sincerely, they worshiped in "the dens and caves of the earth."

From time to time, from the toleration act of Henry of Navarre, there swarmed off from out of the old hive, colonies to other European lands, to the French West Indies, and into the English colonies of America. The stories of disguise and escape across the frontiers, as told in reminiscence around the firesides in the homes of what are now the United States, if written down, would make a volume as thrilling as any of romance.

It was not, however, till after the Revocation in 1685 that the Huguenots of France left by tens of thousands, as exiles, to find homes afar. The British Isles, the Dutch Republic, and the German states were enriched, and so were the West Indies, especially the island of St. Christopher, and South Africa; but not least among those countries that profited most by the immigrations were the English colonies along the Atlantic front.

Into Puritan Massachusetts, into cosmopolitan New Netherland, under the liberal government of William Penn, to the rich soil of Virginia and into the Carolinas — enough almost by themselves to create a commonwealth — they came and with welcome.

In New York there was both scattering and concentration. Into the Long Island and the Hudson River regions, thousands of them went at once for food and shelter, but on the land of Jacob Leisler they made their mark most historic, and there, for numbers, was the largest single permanent colony of the Huguenots in America.

On the site of the Huguenot settlement in 1683 at Oxford, near Worcester, Massachusetts, a memorial in the form of a cross has been reared. Under the persistent attacks of the savages, egged on by influences from Canada, this frontier enterprise was abandoned. Traces of the bastioned fort on the hill remain to suggest that, even as John Robinson, the Pilgrim pastor, taught, the best and the worst may be done in the name of religion.

CHAPTER XXVII

THE AMERICAN WALLOON DOMINES

THE first book in the English language published by a member of the Reformed Church in America was by Reverend Lambertus de Ronde, of Walloon ancestry, whose parents had named him after the celebrated seventh-century saint, whose name is preserved in so many churches in Belgium. He had had several years' experience as a pastor in Surinam, where he became warmly interested in the education of the black slaves. In 1749, he wished to publish in Negro English a "First Book of Christian Truths." In New Netherland, he served churches at New York, Haarlem, and Schaghticoke, New York. In the Revolution, because he was an intense American patriot — as were most ministers of Huguenot or Netherlands ancestry — he was hunted and driven away from his own flock by the British. During this time, he shepherded the churches at Red Hook and Saugerties.

De Ronde translated the Constitution of the United States into Dutch, and possibly also into German, when, of the thirteen States, six had already adopted it. This was done by order of the Federal Committee, and his work was published in Albany in 1788.

De Ronde's career in the Reformed churches was

at a time when in the larger settlements the children of Walloons, Dutch, and Germans were talking English, and the boys, instead of being sent to the Netherlands to be educated, went to Yale or Princeton. The time had come when, for safety and unity of the future United States, there was to be but one spoken language, and the Huguenots, Walloons, and Dutch were among the first, in spite of some opposition from the old folks, to set the good example of assimilation. The project of establishing what became Rutgers College was broached as early as 1763. Its charter was obtained in 1766.

During this epoch, when the unifying influences of the English speech and literature were winning their way, the controversy between the ministers of the Cœtus, or Progressives, and the Conferentia, or Conservatives, rent the churches, French, Dutch, and German, in which worship and sermon were in these languages. Few to-day know even the meaning of these terms. The word Cœtus is not in our dictionary, but comes from the Latin *co*-and *iri* — a coming together, an assembly or company. Conferentia, or conference, tells its own story in its form.

At bottom these terms in their application connoted, relatively, what "Tory" and "Whig," "Continental" and "Loyalist," and the more modern "Home Rule" and "Unionist" signify. Their resultant activities and partisanship sprang from the same convictions and impulses. In church, in education, and in politics, Americans began to think it was high time that the churches, schools, and local government should be free from the direct control of authority across the Atlantic.

In theological education, especially, young men, it was thought, should be trained not in Europe, but in America. Churchmen, educators, and statesmen were all drifting towards unity of opinion in these matters and, whether they knew it or not, towards ultimate independence of lands beyond sea. Yet throughout, there was the deep-seated feeling of loyalty to the Mother Countries.

Yet how?

Surely not to the Europe that was passing away — the old continent of united Church and State, of exclusive Latin culture, of despots on thrones, of antiquated institutions that were but the shreds and patches of mediæval feudalism.

The real deep-seated loyalty was to the best ideas and traditions of ancient freedom and to the nobler principles generated by the Reformation. These Americans were led on by beacon hopes of a better social order, a higher loyalty to their Master and more direct approach to their Creator, to an education that would fit the rising generation for more immediately coping with New World problems. They wished their sons to be trained for such forms of government as would mean less dependence on thrones, worn-out traditions, and absentee rulers, and would more strenuously develop self-rule and fitness to meet the political problems unknown to the Old

World, but insistent on the new continent and immediately confronting themselves.

Dr. Archibald Laidlie, born in Scotland, after serving at Flushing in Zeeland, preached in English in the Reformed Church on Manhattan and revised the English translation of her impressive and beautiful liturgy, as well as the Belgic Confession of Faith, into what was to be the master-speech of the United States and of seven nations and may yet be of the world.

Another of the ministers of Walloon descent in the Reformed Church, who lived to be ninety-two and was in active service during seventy-two years, was Henry Ostrander. Born at Plattekill, near New Paltz, New York, March 11, 1781, he spent most of his life serving churches near those mountains which at sunset throw their shadows on the bosom of the Hudson. Living before the presidency of Washington and until 1872, he linked in his own life two different periods of national life and of language, for he could preach in Dutch or English, and he wrote both in fine, terse style. In him, boldness of spirit and gentleness of manner were combined.

Another minister, probably of the same stock and kindred, Stephen Ostrander, born at Poughkeepsie in 1769, who lived to be seventy, was a pioneer preacher among the Seneca Indians and in the counties that were still mainly forest.

In the Reformed Church in America, in the course of generations, were several notable families of ministers who could preach in both Dutch and French.

THE STORY OF THE WALLOONS

In some cases, those of Dutch, Walloon, or Huguenot stock, within three generations produced a dozen or more ministers or ministers' wives. Not a few of these carried in the very texture of their names, and the meaning of them, the symbols of movement and of elasticity of spirit, even in the midst of gloom and suffering. The name Vermilye, which signifies from, or out of the midst, is a typical instance. Of these, Reverend Thomas E. Vermilye, born on Manhattan in 1803, served from 1839 to 1893, in the line of pastors of the same old "Church in the Fort" of 1628. With the advance of population, the two new edifices for the enlarged congregations are to be seen on the corners of Twenty-ninth Street, and of Forty-eighth Street, on Fifth Avenue.

Reverend Depuytren Vermilye graduated from Rutgers College in 1863. Ashbel G., son of Thomas, born at Princeton in 1822, was pastor at Schenectady, New York, from 1871 to 1876. In a large sense, he was a historian of his people, for his profound and polished paper on "The Huguenot Element in the Reformed Church" is a masterpiece of fine English and of condensed history. In treating of Jacob Leisler, in an essay in "The Memorial History of New York," which shows not only candor, generosity, breadth of mind, a finished style, and judicial poise, he antiquated (while emptying of slander) all previous discussions upon this theme. He exposed the silliness and obscuring prejudice which had so long befogged the subject. Few men in courtesy, wit, and majestic personal appearance were better representatives of the American of Huguenot descent.

It was on the whole a cosmopolitan ministry that served the Reformed Church. In its composition this body of Christians reflected that over-sea Republic which, as the prototype of the American, fed the hungry, helped the needy, and welcomed the oppressed of every land, clime, and creed. We find among the duly educated, university-bred, and regularly ordained pastors within its bounds, men of Swiss, Swedish, Danish, German, French, Walloon, Flemish, Dutch, Scotch, Irish, Welsh, and English birth, besides the many born on American soil. Most of these have shown themselves typical patriots, free from that sectionalism which has thrown its blight over American historiography, making much of our national story a caricature of reality. This latter fact is clear, even in several notable series of volumes from the presses of eminent publishers.

The last student among hundreds to go to Patria, or the Netherlands, for a university education, or for his theology, at Leyden or Utrecht, was John H. Livingston, born at Poughkeepsie in 1746, who was graduated from Yale College. On his return in 1769 he became the virtual founder of two institutions, both at New Brunswick, New Jersey. One of these makes claim to be the oldest Divinity School in America. Rutgers College had already, in 1766, been chartered, but did not begin instruction until 1770. The strong motive underlying its founding was op-

THE STORY OF THE WALLOONS

position to the active propaganda of Anglican State Churchism attempted on and from Manhattan. The sentiment of those who nourished the beginning of Rutgers College was for free choice in religion.

On every one of freedom's battle-fields, from the War of Independence until "the return of the New Netherland" to Europe in 1916, with the American Expeditionary Force, the blood of Alma Mater's sons has crimsoned the soil of America, Asia, and Europe, in making with willingness "the supreme sacrifice." One of the best known of the six hundred forty soldiers from Rutgers and her alumni — four hundred being commissioned officers in the world war — was the promising young poet, Joyce Kilmer. In "the victories of peace no less renowned than war," the children of Rutgers have promptly responded to the nation's call. No college, in proportion to the number of graduates, has sent out so many teachers and pioneers of science and religion to Asia and the East Indies as Rutgers College.

The motto of Utrecht University — a monument of the triumph of the modern ideas of mental freedom over the reactionary despotism of Spain, and also of the victory of Calvinism, with its public schools, over Loyolaism — was *Sol justitiæ illustra nos;* that is, Sun of [Divine] Justice, shine on us (or literally, rise with *healing*). To this, from the Vulgate, Livingston added, in two words, a prayer on behalf of America, *et Occidentem*, or, Sun of Justice, illuminate also the West.

THE AMERICAN WALLOON DOMINES

Rutgers has ever been forward in the new course of empire. During the War of the Revolution, most of the faculty and students were in the Continental army. The first graduate, Simeon de Witt, was on the staff of Washington. He laid out the works at Yorktown, settled the boundaries, and surveyed most of the central area of New York State, when it was chiefly forest land.

More than any other college, Rutgers, "on the banks of the old Raritan," has in the past educated the American sons, and in recent years the daughters, who are descendants of the Walloons and Huguenots. It was into this beautiful river valley that very many of their ancestors emigrated to make their homes, when the English governor Cornbury, of the colony of New York, abused his power.

For David de Forest, the Connecticut pioneer (1669-1721) and the large number of his descendants at Stratford and in the hill towns, and for the record of the de Forests in war time, one must consult the engaging volumes of Mrs. R. W. de Forest, entitled "A Walloon Family in America." In the various local histories of the cities, towns, and villages founded in Nova Belgica, New Netherland, or New York, one will find abundant proofs of the sterling qualities in this strain, which made a decidedly perceptible addition to the American composite. Their full story deserves a far worthier chronicler than the present one, who merely lifts the curtain.

CHAPTER XXVIII
NAMES IN TRANSFORMATION

ONE of the most interesting facts about emigrants is the frequency of their change of names. Done in every age, land, and language — as any one familiar with his Bible knows — it makes many puzzles for the historian.

For these transformations, from Abram to Abraham and from Jacob to Israel, down to Eleazer into Lazarus, Paul from Saul, and Joshua into Jesus, there is a reason, divine or human; but usually the change is made to make life more easy, to save time and trouble in spelling, pronunciation, personal writing, official record, and strain upon the vocal organs. Such a process may also save taxes or shut off too close official inquiry or personal scrutiny. Often the transformation is a memorial of gratitude. Even in modern days, apart from adoption and choosing namesakes, the custom is surprisingly common.

It is laughable, when in the Dutch archives, to scan the lists of betrothals and marriages of the Pilgrims and other Free Churchmen, as written by clerks who knew no English. Yet some of the Pilgrim Fathers took Dutch names, or wrote their autographs in forms easily read or pronounced by the natives, to suit the Dutch ear and eye.

. In the United States, hundreds of names of

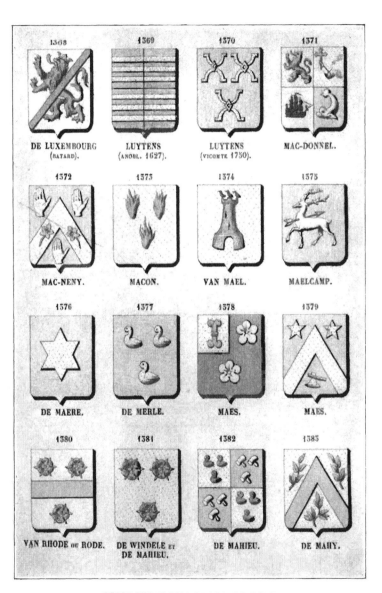

1368	1369	1370	1371
DE LUXEMBOURG (BATARD).	LUYTENS (ANOBL. 1627).	LUYTENS (VICOMTE 1750).	MAC-DONNEL.
1372	1373	1374	1375
MAC-NENY.	MACON.	VAN MAEL.	MAELCAMP.
1376	1377	1378	1379
DE MAERE.	DE MERLE.	MAES.	MAES.
1380	1381	1382	1383
VAN RHODE ou RODE.	DE WINDELE et DE MAHIEU.	DE MAHIEU.	DE MAHY.

SOME WALLOON COATS OF ARMS

NAMES IN TRANSFORMATION

Walloon and French Huguenots, that have passed through the filters of three countries and languages, are almost unrecognizable, even by experts. It is amusing and interesting to compare the various forms of the same patronymic, as it is found in Sweden, South Africa, Spanish South America, Holland, or in the seven countries of English-speaking people. We are reminded of a kaleidoscope, or of Joseph's coat of many colors, or of the old man who heard the voice of Isaac while feeling the hands of Esau. In some cases, the result suggests a crazy quilt. To all these obstacles to correct genealogy is added the anarchy which was prevalent before spelling was harnessed to rules, and when often the same person would write his own name in several different ways.

Let us for our recreation make an excursion into comparative etymology and philology. Belgic Walloons, and French Huguenots usually altered, translated, or transliterated their names, in order to be in harmony with their environment and to save mental, visual, and vocal exertion on the part of their hosts.

In the Dutch Republic, to give a few examples, le Grand became de Groot; Chevalier, de Ruyter; Dumont, van den Berg; du Jardin, Bogaard or Bogart; Dumoulins, van der Meulen, etc.

Other names, recognizable in both Dutch and English, are Barry, Bonheur, Bonny, Donny, Emery, Hardy, Peletier, Brill, Payne, Symonds, Haynes,

Torry, Vincent, and a hundred others we meet with in the telephone directories.

When it comes to the transformations to be noted in English and American, to say nothing of Irish, Scotch, and Welsh forms, which were originally Belgic or French, we may count them by the thousands. Even the ancient and classic names common to all Christendom, such as Alexander and Peter, may by human descent come to us in or from the French form. In fact, personal as well as family appellatives suffered a "sea change" in crossing frontiers, as well as the briny deep. Others in the list below, like Agnew, Astor, Avery, Bailey, Barr, Batchelder, Bean, Benn, Briggs, Chambers, Clark, Coppinger, Crowley, Daggott, Dennis, Driver, Fremont, Goucher, Gray, Hewett, Jackman, Jaspar, Julian, Longfellow, Lovell, Miles, Mott, Neale, Osler, Pillow, Perkins, Patton, Pearse, Pettee, Pickens, Plummer, Powell, Quincy, Ramey, Revell, Rose, Rowland, Seymour, Spicer, Terry, Vernon, Wallers, Dwight (from de Witt), Bumpus (from Bon Repos), etc., etc., though so long naturalized as to seem as if grown on English soil, are the names of refugees from the Low Countries, or France. Most of these had taken their English form before they were known in America.

Of the descendants of the fifteen thousand Walloon or French-speaking Huguenot immigrants in Pennsylvania alone, of Belgic or French stock, probably not more than a small fraction to-day bear the original form of the names borne by their ancestors three centuries ago. The prefixes or suffixes have been dropped apparently without rule or reason.

De Foe's poem on the "True-Born Englishman" finds its counterpart in the United States, where the blood is as mixed as in the Jewish, the French, the English, or any other supposedly "pure" but non-existent race, that has migrated like a plant or animal. The study of names is much like that in qualitative chemistry. On the quantitative side it has been shown, however, that of the hundred or more millions of people in the United States, at least fifty-five millions had American grandfathers born on the soil. Nevertheless, probably with more than half, except in the case of simple words like Smith, Brown, Jones, etc., the orthography of their names differs from that of their ancestors, whether known or unknown. The most ordinary and many of the rare names are like old garden plants that have "escaped from cultivation" and grown wild, developing new features in a new environment.

In the light of this habit, it is easy to accept and believe the persistent and general tradition, held contemporaneously in New York, that Jacob Leisler was the son of a Walloon or Huguenot pastor, who in Frankfort had changed his name, giving it a German form, as did thousands of the refugees, who became even more German than the native born in the Palatinate.

Without pretense of unraveling the many strands

of ancestry, that have entered into the well-woven
texture of the American of Walloon descent, making
him what he is, an alien has the right of giving
the results of observations in the southern Belgic
provinces. Even he can in most cases, among the
peasants at least, discern the differences between
Fleming and Walloon. At the market and in the
fields, in the factories and shops, one has a good
opportunity to study faces, figures, actions, and
speech. The modern Walloon, as I have seen him
at home, is "stocky," thick-set in figure, and of a
swarthier complexion, with blue or brown eyes. He
is more quickly emotional, easily roused, interested,
or excited, but, sooner than the Fleming, regains his
mental equilibrium. Not only in the ditties heard
at labor, but in the talk of men and women, there is
a sort of sing-song cadence. As a rule, the Walloon
creature of either sex is gayer, merrier, and more
prone to extremes in his mirth and pleasures.

In matters of religion, or philosophy, or reform,
the Walloon inclines toward Socialism, but is more
abstract in his ideas than the Fleming. Probably a
majority of the Walloons are out-and-out Socialists
— whether it pays to be such or not. The Flemings
are, in the main, strict Churchmen and their Socialism is wholly practical, hardly rising higher than
successful economics. The Walloon starts things.
He begins heresy, reform, revolution, progress —
whatever may mean new ideas, requiring active
cerebration; but the Fleming, slower in beginning,

NAMES IN TRANSFORMATION

has more tenacity and is more likely to bring to completion whatever he takes hold of.

The Protestants of Belgium, numbering several tens of thousands, are active and increasing; but their field of enterprise seems to be almost wholly in the Flemish provinces. Roughly speaking, there are to-day no Protestant Walloons in southern Belgium.

In all these narratives of the Walloon heroes of faith and freedom, we should not forget the woman by the side of the man, who, with her finer strength, suffered also for conscience' sake.

Neither the Belgians nor the French take kindly to emigration. Perhaps above all others they are tenacious of life on the home soil. Yet with father, husband, brother, and usually burdened with the care of the children, the Walloon maiden, wife, mother, left the old home to go forth, scarcely knowing whither. Not a few instances in the annals of flight and exile are known, where widows or single women, even with little ones, by wit or address or pure valor passed the guards and boundaries on the way to freedom. Nor did they fail, in the new and often forbidding environment, as true helpmates, to adapt themselves to the strange conditions of life in foreign lands.

Even as the fossils found in the rocks and strata of an older world show marvelous modifications, which enabled the once existent organisms to live in harmony with their surroundings, awakening in the scientific mind wonder and admiration, so with the

271

silent records of births, marriages, deaths, and entombment. As we scan the lists on the original parchments, or on the page of reprints, or on the stone covers of the tombs within churches, or on the lichened records in the cemetery, the imagination kindles.

In our own land, the annals of the American colonies or frontiers stir the blood, as we picture the past, or recall what we heard directly from the lips of Revolutionary ancestors, and we scarce wonder at the resurrection of art in tablet affixed, or sculpture upreared — "lest we forget." We welcome the book written or picture painted to save from oblivion the heroic past, which inspires us for present duty.

Equally worthy of remembrance are the heroic Walloons. Surely a virgin field awaits the pen, chisel, and brush of the American who loves the ideal side of life. It is for artist and sculptor to make known in a better way than our feeble pen, a story which, when our American people know it well, they will "not willingly let die," but bring to the resurrection of art for "glory and for beauty."

CHAPTER XXIX

LIFE'S JOURNEY AMONG THE WALLOONS

A CHILD or an alien, journeying in storied lands, may be unmindful of the great events, on consecrated soil, which to the native, or the mature student of history and the man or woman of culture, make their fitting appeal. So also, concerning the Walloons or their country, has been the life experience of many Americans who scarcely know even the meaning of the word, Walloon.

The names herein recorded of friends, schoolmates, companions in play, and of eminent citizens may, to those of English descent, have seemed odd, often interesting in passing thought or even worth inquiring about. Youth, that lives in the hour, makes slight inquest, or none, into the past.

But what pretty faces among the girls, what jolly fellows at school, in sport, under arms, at athletics, and in classroom and picnics! What good society at parties! What level-headed mature men of judgment and kindly presence! What fine old ladies! What pleasant visitors in the home, partners in the joy and grief of common experiences, in the school, church, city, and nation, do some of us recall!

Without fully comprehending heredity or history, we could hardly fail to note the gracious manners and the joyous temperaments in the bearers of these names that sounded so odd. Did we not dimly fancy in these a finer strain than the ordinary?

Such were the Benezets, the Supplees, the Parmenters, the Morrells, du Bosques, Grimms, Santees, Boyers, Hamlins, Bodines, du Boises, Boutons, Cressons, Clements, Bontecous, Cessnas, Boileaus, de Lanceys, Duryeas, la Grands, Forneys, Garrigues, Labaws, Herrings, Lefevres, Markoes, Martines, Ritners, and scores more which memory could recall.

Do not we, grandchildren of the men of 1787, love to remember the gratitude of our fathers, who wrote it in the Constitution that any one, even a foreigner by birth, who was "a citizen of the United States at the time of the adoption of this Constitution" might become President?

Besides the host of descendants, Germans, Swiss, Danes, Netherlanders, Walloons, Flemings, Dutch and French Huguenots, which no man has yet precisely numbered, did we not read and gradually attain to deeper insight into the older street names, which reflect much of the history of our cities by the seaboard, from Boston to Charleston, South Carolina? In the Empire State, even among the mighty multitudes of the "vans" and the "tens," how numerous are those which are telltale of their origin, such as de Forest, Dellamont, Truax, deGraeff, Mabie, Baptiste, Trego, la Grand, Remy and many another, with the prefix "de" or "la" — on or off! Yet all of these named in this book are only a few of the historical prefixes that have survived in the American social climate and usage, for most of our fellow citizens descended from French-speaking forbears have dropped these.

Even in the city dubbed "the Hub" by a Walloon descendant — the great-great-great-grandson of the Schenectady church deacon Wendell — what a revelation! Here were Walloon and Huguenot names galore! The first schoolmaster was Purmort. The chief historic edifice was Faneuil Hall. The rider between the lantern in the church steeple and Lexington Common was Paul Revere! Here dwelt the families, Brimmer, Cabot, Beard, Durant, Dolbear, Leland, Perry, and scores of others more or less famous. Many families of Huguenot blood and faith have become extinct, but their names live. "The cry of the eagle is heard long after his form has disappeared behind the mountain," says the Chinese proverb.

In church, club, market, shop, and store, and in the seats of culture, were numerous descendants of French-speaking ancestors in early New England; while at Plymouth, near by, were fragrant memories of Priscilla Mullens, the typical "Puritan" maiden, who was born in France!

The balance of probabilities visible in 1922 is that John Alden, lover and husband, was also of the same stock and probably by way of North Ireland, or possibly eastern England, to which so many Walloons and French fled in very early days. It is delightful recreation to hunt up in Boston the names and

275

places associated with the Huguenots, and to learn that in the veins of those sweet singers, Longfellow and Whittier, in Thoreau also, and in thousands of "typical" New Englanders, flowed blood of the same strain.

In the archipelago at the mouth of the Hudson River, in the various cities on Long, Staten, Manhattan, and smaller islands, behold the host in the sixth and later generations! All around us are the Disosways, Lispenards, Jays, Motts, Jaudons, Julians, Duvals, and scores, yes, hundreds of names that shed luster on the metropolis of America. In its social *penetralia*, New York is a Walloon-Dutch-Huguenot town.

But why make a prolongation — as of mighty Alpine echoes and resonances from the same little horn of utterance? The identical social phenomena are both audible and visible in the cities, towns, and villages of our forty-eight States. On the shop signs, doorplates, and the "mossy marbles," one reads the names, "carved for many a year" of the Belgic Walloons of Hainault, Namur, Liège, Mons, the Ardennes and of the French cities that were once in Walloon Land, such as Valenciennes, Lille, Béthune, Arras, and Douay.

In the old home lands beyond sea some of us have greeted or shaken hands with Walloon folk, or even been hospitably entertained in homes of culture and refinement, in which dwelt a people bearing the same patronymics as those which, however pronounced

LIFE AMONG THE WALLOONS

differently or expressed in print or writing, or cari-
catured by transforming phonetics, were really the
same as those borne by thousands in America. On
club and church lists, in directories and on the rolls
of fame, we find them.

In addition, there are all around us places known
by record or memorial, the sites of extinct settlements of French people, such, for example, as Oxford (Worcester), Massachusetts; Azilum (Rum-
mersfield), Pennsylvania, and on the map scores of
"French" towns, "French" creeks, "French" hills,
or "French" this or that, and yet many more to be
read about in gazetteers and in forgotten documents.
The "French Blood in the United States" — to
quote the title of Fosdick's fascinating volume, or to
note Finley's "The French in the Heart of America,"
or the books of the Baird brothers — is very far
from being the least element in the American composite. Senator Henry Cabot Lodge finds that no
strain in the American composite has produced
more men and women of note in our country's history.

For one to travel leisurely in the South is simply
to repeat the story of "old experience," and, in this
case also, with great Milton, to "attain to something of prophetic strain." In Virginia and the Carolinas, besides noting the abundance of Ravenels,
Colignys, Gaillards, Gregories, de Veaux, and hearing hundreds more of like formation and lineage,
there may be seen, sprinkled on the pages of city

directories, Huguenot names as plentiful as violets on the perfume farms of sunny France.

Not that a name, or any form of it, can always in itself tell — even if met with in American history before 1800, as truly as a finger print is a sign of individuality — the story of origin, ancestry, language, or country. Nevertheless, the primitive old spelling often affords a helpful and an enlightening clue. To make one wary of pitfalls, one need but think of the avalanche of immigrations from Canada and Europe, the floods from the bayous of Louisiana and the deposits in the northwest from the old French occupation. To the unforewarned researcher, a patronymic with deceitful resemblance, especially in its modern spelling, is much like the pits made by the Walloons on Staten Island. They were covered over with sticks, earth, leaves, or flowers, for wolves to fall in and be trapped.

Set opposite to our immeasurable debt, created by inheritances of language and law and by what Europe brought to us in blood and ideas, is the column of continuous, beneficent American reaction on the old home lands. Great Britain learned from her American experience a noble colonial policy and treatment of races. Franklin taught an over-luxurious court the beauties of the simple life and hinted that ordered liberty was a nation's best strength. Lafayette and the cohorts of French soldiers went back to create a new France, by breaking the yoke of ecclesiastical despotism. Besides striving to mitigate the horrors of the French Revolution — the reaction against the dual despotism of Church and State united — Lafayette strove to gain for his countrymen what he had seen in America, free churchmanship. He did not agitate or labor for mere tolerance, that is, the right to live, but for freedom of conscience for all. By degrees, France won soul liberty by breaking the shackles of the Latin potentate and corporation, even to withdrawing her legation from Rome and severing diplomatic relations with the papal dynasty, and finally, in 1905, ceasing to subsidize any cult. Nothing else so assisted to make of the hero nation the "Eternal France" of 1914 as this action. Later relations with the Vatican were resumed on a new basis. In resisting the Teutonic onslaught of 1914, Jew and Gentile, Catholic and Socialist, Reformed and Unreformed, marched as one man. In a word, France reached and accepted the Huguenot position of the sixteenth century.

Others have told the story of eminent men and women of Walloon stock from the old Belgic Land who won fame in America — though their merit is usually ascribed to inheritances from France. It is not for us, in this volume, to expatiate on what our nation owes to those who bear the names of de Forest, Minuit, Montaine, du Bois, Hillegas, Laurence, Boudinot, Marion, Hamilton, Reynolds, Howe, Bethune, Vassar, Dana, etc., etc., or to enter into the flowery fields of literature, art, eloquence, inven-

THE STORY OF THE WALLOONS

tion, enterprise, and exploration, in order to discover
our debt to the Walloon, or to do what Schiller has
told us, or to sound again the plaudits so deserved.
He may rather draw a parable from Bedloe's Island
in New York Harbor, whereon stands the colossal
statue of "Liberty Enlightening the World." The
initial property of a Walloon, the history of the island was for two centuries or more that of modest
usefulness only. It seemed set in the water for
naught but "homely joys and destiny obscure,"
until grateful France made ready her gift of Bar-
tholdi's artistic triumph.

Nevertheless, Americans tarried in their response
and the fitting pedestal awaited its uprearing until
James W. Pinchot, of Walloon descent, summoned
his fellow citizens to their duty and privilege. Now,
set on high, besides being "a thing of beauty" and
"a joy forever," the electric current, generated from
the long-hidden treasures within the earth, makes
this statue at night a beacon for ships "to give light
and to save life."

"History is a resurrection."

THE END

THE FRAMEWORK OF TIME

THE FRAMEWORK OF TIME

FROM primeval ages, the root form *gal*, or *wal* — as in Gallic *Gaul*, *Galatians*, there being no *w* in Latin, and the letters *g* and *w* being interchangeable in the North — existed in the Indo-Germanic tongues. With the root *oon*, or one, the word "Walloon" was formed and first used in the English language during the sixteenth century; the literal idea of what was stranger, pilgrim, foreign being the same as in "Wales," "walnut," "Wallachia," and in many place-names. Hence *wal*, foreign, *oon*, one = Walloon.

The Coal Forest, once covering a large area in Belgica, over what is now the coal-mining region, was not penetrated by the Romans or Franks, and served as a barrier separating the Belgæ in the south, of Celtic stock, from the Flemings of the north, of Teutonic origin. Hence two races and two languages in Belgium.

In Cæsar's *Commentaries on the Gallic War*, the Belgæ are mentioned as being "the bravest of all these" in Belgica, or "Belgium" — then a geographical term including a great area.

The Roman Occupation.	B.C. 53–A.D. 406
The invasion and empire of the Franks.	A.D. 300
Belgium made part of Austrasia.	511
"The Century of the Saints" — Christian Missionaries.	. 600–700
The Carlovingian Empire.	614–618
Foundation and development of the provinces, of Belgic Land, until the thirteenth century. The Charcoal Forest.	
Church and State united — Charlemagne.	800
The Verdun Compact. Three Realms.	843
Duchy of Lothair and Principality of Liège.	956–1096
The Belgian Crusades.	1096–1270
The Communes.	900–1500
The Belgian Countships.	900–1279
Flourishing of the Cities.	1200–1500
The Burgundian Era (Unification).	1384–1476

THE FRAMEWORK OF TIME

The Renaissance.	1300–1560
The Turks capture Constantinople. Dispersion of the Greek scholars in Western Europe.	1453
Margaret of Austria, Regent of the Netherlands.	1506–1530
Charles V.	1515–1555
The Reformation Era.	1517–1648
Beginnings of the French Reformation.	1523–1530
Revolt against Spanish Rule.	1555–1598
The "Huguenots."	1550
Translation and singing of the Psalms by the French and Walloon Huguenots.	1545
Translation of the Bible into French.	1523–1530
John Calvin, father of public schools and promoter of the first French Protestant colony in America, Brazil.	1536
Huguenot French attempts at Colonization in Florida.	1562–1564
Walloon refugees in England and the Palatinate.	1544–1700
Hedge preaching. Peregrine La Grand.	1560
Guido de Bray.	1540–1567
The Belgic Confession of Faith.	1561
The Edict of Nantes.	1598
Philip II of Spain.	1527–1598
Spanish Invasion, led by the Duke of Alva.	1567
Flight and Dispersion of the Walloons.	1567–1580
Birth of Usselinx, father of the West India Company and of Walloon Colonization in America.	1567
Beginning of the Great Dispersion.	1567
Union of Arras — the Walloon Provinces return to Spanish allegiance.	1578
Principal migrations of the Walloons into the German Palatinate and other Lands o Exile.	1567–1688
Declaration of freedom of conscience, by William of Orange.	1577
Jesse de Forest in Belgic Land.	1576–1615
Jesse de Forest in Leyden.	1615–1623
He enrolls colonists for Virginia.	1621
The Walloon Provinces react toward Spain. "The Spanish Netherlands."	1579–1713

THE FRAMEWORK OF TIME

The English Separatists arrive in Amsterdam.	1593
The Dutch East India Company formed.	1602
Struggle between the Secession (State Right) and Union parties in the Dutch Republic.	1609–1619
Sailing of the Half Moon. Discovery of New Netherland.	1609
The "Pilgrim Fathers" in Leyden (8 nationalities).	1610–1655
Triumph of the Union Cause and National Synod of Dordrecht.	1619
Formation of the Dutch West India Company.	1621
Dutch fur-traders, fishermen, and explorers in New Netherland.	1610–1624
Arrival of the ship New Netherland, with thirty families, mostly Walloons. Founding of New York and the Middle States. The first homemakers and tillers of the soil. Four Walloon married couples settle in the Delaware Valley.	1624
William Verhulst, Director. New settlers arrive, with live-stock, tools, mechanics, etc.	1625
New Netherland, a province of the Dutch Republic, organized with a civil government and seal and named [Terra] Nova Belgica.	1626
First public worship in organized church and preaching to the Walloons in America.	1628
The Austrian Netherlands (Absolutism).	1714–1794
Belgian territory ceded to France and becomes Artois and later Département du Nord.	1668
"A Century of Misery." Belgium "the Cockpit of Europe."	1600–1700
Belgium united to Holland.	1814–1830
Independence of Belgium, the Modern Kingdom, with freedom of conscience.	1830
Formation of Huguenot Societies in U.S.A.	1883
Publication of The de Forests of Avesnes.	1900
Publication of the Poujol's History and Influence of the Walloon Churches in the Netherlands.	1902
The Great World War.	1914–1918
"Return of the New Netherland." American help to Belgium and France.	1916–1918

THE FRAMEWORK OF TIME

Issues of five editions of Corwin's *Manual*, showing Walloon and Dutch pastors.	1859–1922
Publication of *A Walloon Family in America*.	1914
Federal Council of Churches propose a national Tercentenary celebration, in 1924, of the founding in 1624, of New York, by the Huguenot Walloons.	1922

INDEX

INDEX

INDEX

Bontecou, 274.
Boston, 254, 275.
Boudin, 201.
Boudinot, 279.
Boughton, George H., 177.
Bouton, 274.
Boyer, 274.
Bradford, 108, 139, 143, 170, 177, 181, 207.
Branding, 121.
Brazil, 181, 188, 203.
Brethren, The, 56–58. See *Anabaptists*.
Brewer, W., 195.
Brides, 148, 248.
Briggs, 268.
Brill, 103, 267.
Brimmer, 275.
British elements, 245.
Brooklyn, 195.
Brussels, 11, 12, 46.
Bryce, James, 226.
Buddhism, 29, 92.
Bumpus, 268.
Burgundian era, 35–41.
Burnet, Bishop, 222.

Cabot, 275.
Calvin, 62, 69, 72, 118, 132, 187.
Calvinism, 117, 180.
Calvinists, 5, 78, 149.
Cammaerts, 25.
Canada, 5, 152, 153, 186, 242, 248, 253.
Cannibals, 154.
Canterbury, 182.
Carillons, 69, 83.
Carleton, Sir D., 140.
Carolinas, 256, 257, 277.
Carpets, 160.
Catechising, 98, 168, 183, 186.
Cathedrals, 31, 88, 89.
Catholic, 61.

Catskill Mountains, 214, 261.
Cattle, 197.
Cessna, 274.
Chadaine, 201.
Chaillé, 201.
Chambers, 268.
Champlain, 153.
Changes in names, 266–72.
Charlemagne, 19, 20, 164.
Charles II, 42–50.
Charles V, 42–50.
Charles the Bold, 38, 39, 271.
Charleston, 254.
Charters, 46.
Chevalier, 267.
China, 135.
Chinese, 21, 22, 31, 32, 275.
Christianity, 74.
Christine, 116.
Christmas, 205, 206.
Church and State, 19, 20, 40, 94, 99, 146, 207, 220, 223, 227, 229, 230, 260, 279.
Church charters, 229.
Church edifices, 164, 174, 205.
Churches, 89–100.
Church government, 89–100.
Church in the Desert, 256.
Church in the Fort, 163, 189.
Church records, 204.
Church under the Cross, 92, 94, 105.
Cities in U.S.A., 274.
City republics, 36.
Civilizations, 137, 138, 160, 164.
Clarks, 268.
Cleanliness, 197.
Coal forest, 23, 26, 27, 196.
Cocceius, 238, 239.
Cockeran, 238, 240.
Cockpit of Europe, 37, 89.
Coetus and Conferentia, 259.
Coins, 132, 171.

290

INDEX

Coleman, C. A., 240.
Coligny, 131, 132, 277.
Colonization, 99, 138.
Colonization of America, 5, 131, 132, 134, 148, 159–61.
Colonizers of America, 64, 66, 116, 130, 159–61.
Consistory, 77, 78.
Constitution, 274.
Coppinger, 268.
Courtrai, 36.
Cradles, 157, 158, 168.
Crefeld, 210.
Cremation, 154.
Crescent. See *Half Moon.*
Crockerton, 203.
Crowley, 268.
Cruller, 171.
Cubberlys, 203.

Daggott, 268.
Daillé, P., 204, 205.
Daisy. See *Marguerite.*
Dana, 279.
Danes, 75, 196.
d'Athenus, 79.
Dathenus, P., 79, 96–98.
de Besche, 112, 113.
de Bres, G. See *Guido de Bray.*
Decoration, interior, 159, 161.
Defoe, 269.
de Forest, David, 265.
de Forest, Jesse, 134–40, 144, 165, 194.
de Forest, Rachel, 194.
de Forest, Mrs. R. W., 134, 265.
de Forests, 75, 76, 274.
de Geer, 111–14.
de Graeff, 274.
de Groot, 22, 267.
d'Iberville, 254.
de Laet, 193.
de Lanceys, 274.

Delaware, 110, 115, 116, 174.
Delfshaven, 98, 139.
Dellamont, 274.
Democracy, 78, 130.
Denmark, 118, 196.
Dennis, 268.
Département du Nord, 9, 11, 248, 251, 253.
Depew, 201.
Depres, 69.
de Rasieres, 166–182.
de Reus, 195, 197.
de Ronde, Lambertus, 258.
de Rosen, 128.
de Ruyter, 267.
de Veaux, 277.
de Witt, Simeon, 265.
Dexter, H. N., 186.
Dey, D. J., 196.
Dikes, 106.
Disosways, 201, 203, 276.
Distinctive America, 3, 151.
Doctrines, 56, 57.
Documents, 117.
Dolbear, 275.
Domine, 158, 188, 189, 190, 239.
Domines, 239, 258–65.
Dordrecht, Synod of, 98–100, 137.
Driver, 268.
Dublin, 104.
Du Bois, 202, 212, 219, 274.
Duché, 201.
du Jardin, 267.
Duke of York, 221.
Dumont, 267.
Dumoulins, 267.
Dunkirk, 142.
Durant, 275.
Duryea, 274.
Dutch and English languages, 259, 261.
Dutch and French speech, 261.
Dutch in America, 114, 115, 116.

INDEX

Dutch Republic, 61, 85, 104, 108, 129, 135, 138, 166, 169, 199, 206, 229, 249, 263.
Dutch traits, 138.
Duval, 276.
Dwight, 268.

East India Company, 134.
Eckhof, Dr., 128, 180, 190.
Economics, 103, 117, 124–29, 233, 251, 252.
Education, 189, 259, 260, 263. See *Catechisms.*
Elector, Frederick William, 94, 95, 211, 220.
Emblems, 87.
Emden, 93.
Emery, 267.
Empire State, 163, 170, 189, 221, 222, 245, 257, 265, 274.
Engagés, 252.
England, 36, 52, 159, 161, 245.
England, Walloons in, 102.
English, 200.
English Conquest, 222, 235.
English Governors, 224.
English speech and literature, 259, 261.
Episcopal Churches, 104, 174, 229, 235.
Erasmus, 49.
Esopus, 214.
Europe, 260.
European inheritances, 161, 260.
Evangeline, 210.
Evolution, 157, 215.
Explorers, 203.

Farel, 62.
Farms, 192, 197.
Federalism, 104, 106, 135.
Feudalism, 24, 35, 40, 260.
Fillmore, Millard, 153.

Finances, 171.
Firearms, 145, 153, 154, 157, 217.
Firewater, 216, 217.
First Church in New York, 163.
First colonists, 147.
Five Nations. See *Iroquois.*
Flagg, Ernest, 209.
Flags, 3, 4, 5, 95, 104–07, 141, 142, 240.
Flanders, 74.
Flax, 33, 169.
Fleming and Walloon, 270.
Flemings, 8, 19, 101, 197.
Fletcher, Governor, 230.
Florida, 70, 83.
Flushing, 261.
Food, 160, 161.
Forbes, Jeanne A., 240.
Forests, 192.
Forney, 274.
Fort Amsterdam 144, 178.
Fort Orange, 152.
Fosdick, 277.
France, 9, 59, 60, 61–65, 90, 160, 203, 205, 243, 253, 255, 279.
Frankenthal, 212.
Frankfort, 82, 97, 236, 237, 269.
Franklin, B., 229.
Fredericia, 118.
Frederick William, Elector, 127, 128.
Free Churchmen, 132, 227, 266.
Freedom of religion, 245.
Freeman, E. A., 226.
Free Printing, 228.
Fremont, 268.
French, 10, 59, 159, 189, 203, 251.
French Revolution, 121, 122.
Friends, 55.
Frontier influence, 161.
Frontier theory, 224.
Frontiers, 112, 197, 242.

292

INDEX

INDEX

INDEX

295

INDEX

INDEX

297

INDEX

298

INDEX